THE APOSTLE OF TENNESSEE

TL&H TRUTHS, LIES, AND HISTORIES OF NASHVILLE

TRUTHS, LIES, AND HISTORIES OF NASHVILLE

Betsy T. Phillips, *series editor*

As a lead-up to Nashville's 250th anniversary in 2029, Vanderbilt University Press is publishing an ambitious new series consisting of twenty-five small volumes designed to bridge the gap between what scholars and experts know about the city and what the public thinks it knows. These are the stories that have never been told, the truths behind the oft-told tales, the things that keep us in love with the city, and the parts of the past that have broken our hearts, with a priority on traditionally underrepresented perspectives and untold stories.

THE APOSTLE OF TENNESSEE

THE INDEFATIGABLE LIFE & MINISTRY OF FATHER ALOYSIUS ORENGO

JOE PAGETTA

VANDERBILT UNIVERSITY PRESS
Nashville, Tennessee

Published 2026 by Vanderbilt University Press.

Library of Congress Cataloging-in-Publication Data

Names: Pagetta, Joe, 1972- author
Title: The apostle of Tennessee : the indefatigable life and ministry of Fr. Aloysius Orengo / Joe Pagetta.
Other titles: Truths, lies, and histories of Nashville v. 3. (bcp47)
Description: Nashville, Tennessee : Vanderbilt University Press, [2026] | Series: Truths, lies, and histories of Nashville ; vol 3 | Includes bibliographical references and index.
Identifiers: LCCN 2026006430 (print) | LCCN 2026006431 (ebook) | ISBN 9780826500410 paperback | ISBN 9780826500427 epub | ISBN 9780826500434 pdf
Subjects: LCSH: Orengo, Aloysius, 1820-1909 | Catholic Church--Clergy | Catholic Church--Tennessee--History | Missionaries--Tennessee | Tennessee--Church history--19th century | LCGFT: Biographies
Classification: LCC BV3705.O74 P34 2026 (print) | LCC BV3705.O74 (ebook) | DDC 266/.209768--dc23/eng/20260401
LC record available at https://lccn.loc.gov/2026006430

For Keri, Elena, and Pinuccia

CONTENTS

It is painful to reflect on the situation of those Catholics who seek for the bread of life and there are but a few to break it for them.

—*United States Catholic Miscellany*, March 1, 1828

I work for my Master, Jesus Christ; for Him alone I lead a life full of hardships. Let others struggle for the good things in life: let others enjoy them. As for me, I have decided to spend my days unknown in some obscure corner to sacrifice my wretched life for the salvation of souls.

—Fr. Roberto de Nobili, SJ (1577–1656)

Ah, well, that is a missionary's life. To plant where another shall reap.

—Willa Cather, *Death Comes for the Archbishop*

PREFACE

I am what's called a cradle Catholic. I was born into the faith, in a neighborhood in Jersey City, New Jersey, with largely other Catholics, mostly first, second, and third generation Americans. My family's life revolved around our local parish, St. Nicholas, which was only a few blocks away. I went to school at St. Nicholas Grammar School and served as an altar boy in the church from fifth to eighth grade. My mother—and myself and brother and sister when we got older—volunteered to work the church bazaar and bingo nights. I remember vividly the night our monsignor was robbed carrying the till from bingo back to the rectory. An off-duty police officer working security got shot in the leg during the ordeal, but he still chased the robbers through the neighborhood right past our front door. I found the blood trail in the morning.

I went to an all-boys Catholic high school, and eventually, a Catholic college—neither farther than a bus ride from the two-family house we shared with my grandparents.

Growing up Catholic is a little like growing up Italian American. Or growing up in New Jersey or wherever else you're from. It's who you are and not something you think about much, until you get older and start to worry that you're forgetting who you are. It's easy to take these things for granted. It wasn't until I moved to Nashville in the late 1990s that I realized not everyone was Catholic, and that the people in Nashville who *were* Catholic weren't necessarily the Italian American brand of Catholic I was, full of our obsession with iconography, saints, and feast days (and pastries and superstitions and hand gestures). While there were Catholic churches in my new city, they didn't feel the same as the ones in my old one. I realized rather quickly that my faith could no longer be a passive part of my life. It could no longer merely be a cultural touchpoint. When food is an important part of your culture, and there's not a restaurant that serves it where you live, you learn how to cook.

So I doubled down, you might say. I not only rediscovered my Catholic traditions; I worked hard to understand them. I paid attention to the church's liturgical calendar. I read the masters of Catholic writing: Thomas Merton, Dorothy Day, Walker Percy, Graham Greene, Evelyn Waugh, and Toni Morrison (to name a few). I studied the spiritual directions of St. Ignatius while on retreats. I'd been a writer my whole life but now found renewed vigor as a "Catholic writer."

I prayed.

At some point along the way I started to wonder what it must be like when something you love so dearly, something you find so life-giving, is not available to you. What happens when there is a not a Catholic Church a few blocks away; when there is not a priest readily available to celebrate mass for you, to offer you communion, to baptize you or marry you or hear your confession? How do you maintain your faith? And then the COVID-19 pandemic came, and for a while we couldn't celebrate mass with our community. When we finally could, we were still afraid. On Easter Sunday of 2020, my wife, mother-in-law, daughters, and I got dressed in our Easter best and sat on the couch in front of the television in the living room to watch a livestream of the Easter mass from an empty Cathedral of the Incarnation in downtown Nashville. "It is a sad and beautiful world," to quote Roberto Benigni's character in Jim Jarmusch's film *Down by Law*.

Tennessee was late to the influx of Catholic immigrants that populated the Northeast or Maryland, or the deeper southern states of Louisiana and Mississippi. The few Catholics scattered throughout the state were ministered to only occasionally by missionary priests who traveled by horseback from Kentucky. It is believed that Hugh Rogan, who arrived in Middle Tennessee in 1780 after working as a surveyor for the Continental Army, did not see a priest for fifty years. Even when Nashville became a diocese in 1837, it was mostly an aspirational exercise. There weren't many Catholics to minister to, and few priests to minister to them. What was it like for those Catholics? How did they sustain their faith? And what was it like for those priests? As a Catholic writer and historian, my interest was piqued.

The more I explored Tennessee's Catholic history, one name continually came up: Fr. Aloysius "Luigi" or "Louis" Orengo, a remarkable and indefatigable nineteenth-century Italian Dominican missionary priest who served the state for twenty-five years and "has few parallels in the Catholic history of the country," as one historian put it.[1] The same historian, writing in the early twentieth century, noted that he had heard regret from many people that Orengo's story had never been told.[2]

It seemed like divine providence: an Italian immigrant, in Tennessee, whose life had never been told. I had my man: the lens through which I might satisfy my curiosity and explore the state's Catholic history. There was only one problem. As Fr. Victor F. O'Daniel notes in his book, *The Apostle of Kentucky*, "The Dominicans, the world over, are noted for their scant care in making and preserving chronicles in regard to their own works."[3] Orengo's life wouldn't be easy to piece together. I had some work to do.[4]

As a second-generation Italian American, adding to the scholarship and accomplishments of Italians in America (and cutting down the Hollywood stereotypes) has always been a priority for me. Being able to note their contributions to Tennessee, a state not synonymous with Italian achievement, was a bonus opportunity.

My father was twenty-nine years old when he emigrated from Italy to the United States. Orengo was twenty-five when he left Italy and twenty-eight when he arrived in Tennessee. I was twenty-six when I moved from Jersey City, New Jersey, to Nashville. It's a stretch to think our journeys were in any way similar. We lived completely different lives in different times—albeit as idealistic, and maybe a little naïve, relatively young men trying to find our way.

Finally, a note on fact and fiction and truth and lies. In August 2024, I had lunch at a Mexican restaurant in Dickson, Tennessee, with Dr. Kristen Bradley, professor of English at the Humphreys County campus of Nashville State Community College. She got the huevos rancheros with spicy sausage; I got the fajitas. Kristen grew up in McEwen, Tennessee, attended St. Patrick's Catholic Church and School, and wrote her graduate school dissertation on St. Patrick's Annual Irish Picnic. We got to talking about weather lore and the belief that in 170 years it had never rained on the Irish Picnic. Whether it had or hadn't didn't matter to Kristen. What interested her most was why the community at St. Patrick's tells the story that it hadn't rained. Her theory had to do with how hard everyone worked and how dedicated they were in not letting the rain ever get in the way of the event. Basically, because the event had never been canceled, surely it must have never rained. There is a different truth at play here, far more important than the historical weather forecast. What she said changed my thinking about this book.

Certainly, my goal was to tell the most accurate story of Fr. Orengo's life and time in Tennessee. I stopped fixating, however, on whether what I read in oral histories was factual and started thinking instead about where they fit in the overall truth of Fr. Orengo. "To the Catholic writer," wrote Sigrid Undset in her 1942 essay, "Truth and Fiction," "the whole world of facts and truths behind facts will appear in relation to the Ultimate Origin from which everything emanates."[5] I think the reason J. R. R. Tolkien—a Catholic writer himself—has Gandalf tell Bilbo Baggins in *The Hobbit* that "all good stories deserve embellishment" is not because the stories are not good enough themselves, but that Bilbo is far too removed from the accomplishments of his Great-Great-Great-Great-Uncle Bullroarer Took to truly understand their significance. Took's truth, however, remains. He accomplished great things under impossible circumstances.

As Kristen and I were talking about this, the sky opened up on what was an otherwise hot and sunny day. It started pouring rain.

ACKNOWLEDGMENTS

Dr. Kristen Bradley, whom I write about in the preface, was one of the many kind and generous people I met on my journey to tell Fr. Orengo's story. I would like to thank her, and the rest of them, here.

I'm indebted first to those writers and historians who came before me, and whose work I leaned on heavily. There are many, but I'm especially grateful for Fr. Victor O'Daniel, Fr. George Flanigen, Thomas Stritch, Msgr. Owen Campion, and Robin Hood, Farrer Hood Cusomato, and Whit Stiles.

Deacon Mike Wilkins at Holy Rosary Church in Donelson, executive director of Calvary Cemetery in Nashville, was the first person I met with when I started researching this book. I'm thankful for his generosity and knowledge. Sister Mary Esther Potts, OP, librarian at Aquinas College in Nashville, kindly carried out boxes of Fr. George Flanigen's files for me every time I visited the library, even when I had no idea initially what I was looking for. Brent Weibe, archivist for the Diocese of Nashville, shared my enthusiasm for history and answered my text messages any time I sent them, as did his successor, Erica Beatey. I'm also thankful for Tim Tomes, archivist at the Archdiocese of Louisville, and Fr. Gregory Schnakenberg, OP, Provincial Archivist at the Dominican Province of St. Joseph in Washington, DC, whose sharing with me of an exhaustive collection of documents pertaining to Fr. Orengo gave me the early vote of confidence I needed. Thank you to Fr. Augustin Laffay, OP, Archivist General of the Order of Preachers, Curia Generalizia dei Domenicani at

Santa Sabina on Aventine Hill in Rome; Lorri Skelton, Archives Director / Certified Archives Manager of Madison County Public Records at the Madison County Archives in Jackson, Tennessee; and Dr. Fabiana Spinelli, Historical Archivist of Santa Maria Sopra Minerva in Rome, Italy, who translated documents when I asked and exhibited a kindness across continents I am truly thankful for. Fr. Massimo Mancini OP, helped me understand the significance of Fr. Samuel Mazzuchelli and the great responsibility we have when interpreting history. Lindsay Hager and Gordon Belt at the Tennessee State Library & Archives always welcomed me when I made the lunchtime walk across Bicentennial Capitol Mall State Park to the library from the Tennessee State Museum.

In addition to Dr. Kristen Bradley at St. Patrick's in McEwen, I'm thankful to Mike Bradley and the incredible Barbara Hooper, who shared their time and love of their parish with me. Special thanks to Humphreys County Museum director Ted Rice, who closed up his flower shop on a moment's notice to take me to the Museum and tell me all about Humphreys County. At St. Philip Catholic Church in Franklin, I'm thankful to Kim Leisinger, who let me into the chapel so I could say a prayer in one of the churches Fr. Orengo built; to Linda Quezada, who gracefully juggled numerous email exchanges with me to find a time I could visit; and Fr. Ed Steiner, who shared his love of history with me over a lunchtime meal and will always have a place in my heart for the time he served as pastor at the Cathedral of the Incarnation where I attended mass with my mother every Sunday for many years. At St. Mary of the Seven Sorrows in downtown Nashville, I'm grateful for the assistance of Fr. Jayd Neely and Melissa Johnson; and at St. Peter's in Memphis, I appreciated the enthusiasm of Patricia Dres, Lori O'Connor, and Fr. John Lydon, OP.

Deacon Mike Wilkins, Fr. Ed Steiner, and just about anyone else in Nashville that I mentioned this book to said I needed to speak to Msgr. Owen Campion, former Diocese of Nashville pastor, current staffer at Our Sunday Visitor, and Catholic historian. His dissertation on the history of the Diocese in Nashville, archived at the Tennessee State

FIGURE 0.1. The author (left) and Msgr. Owen Campion, historian and current columnist for Our Sunday Visitor. Photo courtesy of Larry McCormack.

Library & Archives, proved invaluable. Even more valuable were the many conversations I had with Msgr. Campion, whether over the phone or over breakfast. He is a treasure.

I'm grateful for the wisdom and expertise I received from Drs. Amie Thurber and Learotha Williams at the Robert Penn Warren Place of Memory Workshop for Middle Tennessee Public Historians at Vanderbilt University and to Elizabeth Meadows and Terry Tripp at the Robert Penn Warren Center for hosting the event and inviting me to attend.

Mahasweta Panigrahy and Eric Sean Amos at the Tennessee Language Institute at the University of Tennessee assisted in getting writings from Orengo, his peers and others translated from Italian and French into English.

I wouldn't have written this book if it hadn't been for Betsy Phillips at Vanderbilt University Press. Spend five minutes with Betsy, and whatever you were curious about when you started, you'll be obsessed with when you finish. Her insatiable curiosity is infectious. How lucky I am that she was my acquisitions editor. She believed I could tell this story and then helped me make it happen. Gianna Mosser, director of Vanderbilt University Press, also helped me make it happen by asking me, every time she saw me, about my writing practice and my writing progress. She knows well the ratio of inspiration and perspiration that goes into writing a book. She's also Italian American and from New Jersey. We speak the same language. A note of gratitude to VUP copyeditor Joell Smith-Borne for her expertise and guidance while polishing this book, and patience with a writer who had never written anything like it before.

I'm privileged to spend my days at the Tennessee State Museum, where I work among gifted history and writing colleagues who offered valuable support during this project. Both Richard White, chief curator, and Dr. Miranda Fraley Rhodes, assistant chief curator, gave me historical context and directed me to resources. I'm especially thankful to executive director Ashley Howell, who encouraged my writing this book, and to Jeff Sellers, my friend and favorite historian, who continually gave me perspective and helped me flesh out my story on lunchtime runs as part of a two-man Tennessee State Museum Run Club. The occasional after-work bourbon and cigar with Jeff was also helpful.

Jeff was an early reader of this manuscript, as was Dr. Kristen Bradley, my dear friend and brother David Fioccola, and my wife, Keri Pagetta (who reads everything I write before it leaves the house).

Thank you to Brother Raymond Murphy of the De LaSalle Christian Brothers, who introduced me to history and museums and culture before I even entered Hudson Catholic High School and remains a dear friend and confidant to this day. I was fortunate to work on edits for this book during a visit with Bro. Ray at the Christian Brothers Residence at La Salle College Prep High School in Philadelphia in the late winter of 2025. Thank you to Fr. Bruce Morrill, SJ, my spiritual director, who listened to me talk about this book for a long time and offered me context whenever I needed it, and to Fr. John Sims Baker and the loving community at Holy Rosary Catholic Church in the Donelson area of Nashville.

To my late father, Ettore, who immigrated to America at age twenty-nine; my mother, Antonia, whose faith exceeds all of ours and whom I know is very proud of me; and my sister, Mary, who's my biggest fan and never lets me forget where I come from—this book is for all of you.

I started researching and writing this book in the late summer of 2023, at about the same time that my mother-in-law, Madge, who had lived with my family for many years, was diagnosed with cancer. While I worked on my book, Madge worked on her life, and then eventually, her death. She passed away at home with us on May 3, 2025, with her children, son- and daughters-in-law, and grandchildren surrounding her with love. I like to think that when she got to heaven, she met Fr. Orengo and said, "Oh, you're the guy! My son-in-law is writing a book about you. We're tired of hearing about it!" I love you, Madge.

My greatest thanks go to Keri and my daughters Elena and Pinuccia, who together with Madge put up with endless dinner conversations in the early days of the book about what I discovered about Fr. Orengo that day. You know you're making an impression, I guess, when your seven-year-old casually asks you over dinner one night, "How's your research on Fr. Orengo going, Dad?" I'm especially grateful for their understanding on all those nights and weekends I disappeared into the home office with a haughty exclamation of "I'm going in!"

Introduction

Leaps and Bounds

For a good image of what it was like to be a Roman Catholic missionary priest in rural middle America in the middle-to-late nineteenth century, look no further than the classic 1970s American television show *Little House on the Prairie*. In episode 6 of the first season, a missionary Catholic priest referred to as Fr. Gorman (played by Henry Olek) arrives on horseback in Walnut Grove, Minnesota, from Mankato, the nearest big city, to preside over the wake and funeral of the very-much-alive Irish immigrant and Catholic Miss Amy O'Hara Hearn.[1] Dressed all in black and in a Roman collar, with a wide-brimmed hat covering his head, Fr. Gorman is sweaty and weary from his two-day journey. His feet are flailing out of the stirrups. He is barely able to keep steady on his horse as he wobbles into town. It's a charming and sympathetic portrait of what missionary priests might have gone through to minister to the scattered faithful. But that's where the comparisons with the fictitious Fr. Gorman and the real-life Fr. Aloysius Orengo end. It's hard to imagine Orengo ever weary; ever wobbling anywhere. He was the very definition of "indefatigable," a word that two newspapers reporting on his travels at the time used for him.[2]

There is a legend that says the first time or two in 1846 that the Italian Dominican priest, who preferred to go as Louis or Luigi, celebrated mass at Saint Dominic's in Springfield, Kentucky, he did not notice the steps leading up to the pulpit from the nave side of the communion rail, which separates the nave from the sanctuary. He placed one foot on the railing and projected himself into the pulpit, so effortlessly that the feat was hardly noticed.[3] Orengo descended from the pulpit by jumping back directly into the sanctuary.

"He could clear any fence without the least difficulty," noted a priest years later who Orengo had mentored. "He would frequently step over the altar railing rather than walk to the gate."[4]

Orengo evaded thieves on the stagecoach road heading west from Nashville by pretending his horse belonged to "his lordship," nearly blinding the would-be thieves by tricking them into looking at the sun. He escaped from soldiers guarding a road during the Civil War by insisting that if they delayed him, they would be responsible for a man dying without last rites. When they went to check with their commanding officer, Orengo escaped into a field of tall corn.

Orengo slept in the woods, used his saddle for a pillow and saddle-blanket for warmth. He sustained himself on cheese and crackers, cornbread and bacon. To his horse, he fed corn. He traveled hundreds of miles to serve the Catholics dotted throughout the region.

When he wasn't traveling by stagecoach or horseback all over Tennessee—he called the trip from the north of the state to the south "my short ride"—he took the evolving railroad. The operators he befriended let him travel in the caboose. When they'd reached the end of a line, Orengo often had to walk to his destination. One retired rail worker, writing from an aging mason's home in Kentucky nearly fifty years after the Civil War, recounted how he offered Orengo his Derringer pistol for safety, but Orengo refused. When he no longer saw him after the war started, the worker feared he had been murdered. "I loved him," he wrote.[5]

Orengo simply could not sit still; not at sixteen years old in 1836 when he traveled south from his home in the Imperia province of northern Italy to enter the Dominicans in Rome; not at twenty-five years old in 1844 when he immigrated to the United States with other Dominicans, including the notable Rev. Sadoc Vilarrasa, who would later found the Dominican Province of the Holy Name in California; not at twenty-seven years old as he preached in Kentucky, leaping into pulpits and complaining to his prior provincial that he wanted to be a missionary and was being forced to live like a monk; nor in the nearly thirty years that followed as he served under three bishops in the Diocese of Nashville and traveled all over Middle and West Tennessee establishing missions, purchasing land, erecting new churches, and getting established churches out of debt. He's credited with building churches in Franklin, Columbia, Pulaski, East Nashville, Tracy City, Gallatin, Humboldt, Brownsville, Grand Junction, Covington, and Jackson. His most notable feat was the thriving Irish Catholic community he helped establish in McEwen, Tennessee, an accomplishment noted with a historical marker erected by the State of Tennessee in 2020. It is in McEwen that Orengo's leadership best embodies my favorite interpretation of what happens during the New Testament story of the miracle of the loaves and fishes and the feeding of the five thousand. In the Gospel of Mark's telling of the story, the disciples are flummoxed over how to serve the thousands that are assembled, thinking the only solution is to purchase the food themselves. Jesus offers another solution. "How many loaves do you have? Go and see," he tells the disciples. When they report back that they have five loaves of bread and two fish, he offers directions on what to do with it. To organize themselves and create a plan of action, they had to first assess what they had to work with and go from there. In McEwen, Orengo informed them that they had each other, ample land, a work ethic, and their faith. Soon, they would have the railroad.

Orengo seems to have baptized about every Catholic child and adult convert (of which he made many) in Middle and West Tennessee. Among them was the infant John Morris, who would grow up to be the Bishop of the Diocese of Little Rock, Arkansas, and a six-month-old African American girl enslaved by Francis Rogan, the youngest son of Hugh Rogan, credited with likely being the first Irish Catholic to settle in the region in the late 1700s.[6]

While he was of a lovable disposition and very much liked by the people, he wasn't always met with open arms by non-Catholics the way the fictitious Fr. Gorman was welcomed in Walnut Grove. While frontier influences had mostly dissipated in Nashville by the mid-nineteenth century, there remained in the city and more so in the rural areas some of its intolerance, bigotry, and theological conservatism.[7] One Baptist minister at the time preached that the Roman Catholic Church maintained its membership by enslaving infants.[8] A prominent Methodist believed the Catholic Church substituted the pope for an emperor, Jesuits for the Apostles, and worshipped images of saints as heathen idols.[9] That kind of talk could have a defensive effect on people. Orengo was once chased away with a butcher knife by the Protestant wife of an Irish Catholic immigrant.[10] Anti-Catholic fervor reached a fever pitch by the mid-1850s when the immigrant faithful appeared to no longer be fellow Christians of another denomination, but foreign agents intent on infiltrating the nation.[11] It was then that Protestant nativism coalesced in the rise of the national anti-immigrant and anti-Catholic Know-Nothing Party.

While the frontier ethos could be a hindrance to educational and cultural progress, it also likely worked to Orengo's benefit. He exemplified the American frontier values of rugged individualism and self-reliance, often carrying stones and bricks to build churches right alongside his congregation. He adapted and innovated where necessary and remained optimistic until his very last days in Tennessee. He believed that the Catholics in Tennessee, like the Americans pushing ever further west, could share destinies.

Even after he returned for good to his native Italy in 1873, Orengo continued his life of service. He joined young men in carrying stones himself to build a church and later ministered to the sick at a former leprosarium back in his home region of Liguria in the Imperia province.

Beyond the leaps and bounds and myths and legends, Orengo was, first and foremost, "abstentious and ascetic, the kind of man of which saints are made," according to a parish historian in 1909, and one of "God's true ministers, following in the footsteps of the Lord," according to a Dominican Sister who had worked with him to establish a school in Jackson, Tennessee, in 1860.[12] Wrote Sister Mary Pius in a 1909 letter:

> "(He was) poor, humble, simple and obedient as a child. He never thought of his comfort, many times, tired, hungry and nowhere to lodge because he did not want to be at a boarding house. He stood as one of God's most saintly messengers. He never lost the spirit of the true religious. His zeal for souls made him forgetful of himself . . . often needing what was necessary, just so he could live and be able to do his work was all he desired. . . A faithful servant, and zealous priest and true religious sums up his character."

In the appendix of his definitive 1926 biography of Nashville's first bishop, Richard Pius Miles, Fr. Victor O'Daniel included brief sketches of priests who figured prominently in the life of the bishop and the diocese. Of Orengo he wrote, "We have heard more than one regret that (Orengo's) life has not been written, for it would make a story of intense interest."

It is that sentence, written almost one hundred years ago, that has most inspired this book. Who was this poor, humble, zealous, and indefatigable servant? What inspired him to travel so far from his home in Italy to be a Catholic missionary in a young country and even younger state? What sustained him in a new and scrappy diocese made up of a relatively small population of Catholics, most of whom were poor immigrants? Where did he find the faith and the fortitude—and the faithful the faith in him—so that the Catholic history of Tennessee could not be written without him?

What's clear again and again in letters and histories is that Orengo was loved by those he served, and that he loved them back, even when they didn't understand what he was saying.[13] It's true, also, whether it was McEwen, or Jackson, or Franklin, that Orengo loved Tennessee. In letters written back to former parishioners and friends in Tennessee after he returned to Italy, he wrote of his longing to return. That love, however, by 1885, almost twelve years after leaving the state, led to heartbreak. The many parishes and missions he helped establish were struggling. "I wish I could be with you in Humboldt and repair and serve your little church," he wrote to Jennie Russell in April of that year, "but I am 65 years old and of little use in America."[14]

Four months later, he responded to a letter from Jennie's younger brother, Johnnie Russell, who had written earlier in the summer and updated Orengo on the status of some of his former parishioners: "The news . . . you give me are very sad to me for I did love the people of my old missions, and it grieves me very much to hear of the misfortunes which happened to some of them . . . I like to know more about the Catholics of Humboldt, Brownsville and Grand Junction and how (they) are carrying on their church, if they have a priest attending to them at least occasionally; my other missions in Middle Tenn., Columbia, Pulaski, Franklin, and Gallatin I fear are also neglected; I have been forgotten by my old friends."[15]

The Catholics in Franklin certainly did not forget him. In 2010 the Williamson County Historical Society acknowledged Orengo's role in establishing St. Philip's Church in 1871 by placing a historical marker in front of the church. In McEwen, Barbara Hooper, director of the St. Vincent de Paul Society Conference at St. Patrick's, keeps his memory alive every day with her zealous spirit and desire to serve the poor. The parish's Irish Picnic each July, instituted by Orengo back in the mid-1850s to raise money for the church's new bell, is still going strong and now raises money for St. Patrick's school.

Orengo may have felt forgotten, but his impact on Catholics and the Catholic faith in Tennessee, is indisputable. Orengo arrived in Tennessee in 1848, slightly more than ten years after the establishment of the Diocese of Nashville, when Bishop Miles could point to six churches and 1,500 Catholics in the entire state. As of this writing, there are a combined 106 parishes in Middle and West Tennessee that serve 146,000 Catholics. Dozens of those parishes can trace their humble beginnings to the tireless and heroic efforts—you might even call them "Herculean"—of a zealous itinerant and beloved Italian Dominican missionary priest who dashed into Nashville on horseback more than 175 years ago.[16]

CHAPTER 1

From Italy to Kentucky

Giacomo Orengo was born to Luigi and Bianca (maiden name Rebaudi) Orengo on January 15, 1820, in the commune of Castel Vittorio, in the Province of Imperia, in the Liguria region of what is now northwestern Italy but at the time was the Kingdom of Piedmont-Sardinia. He was baptized the very next day with his maternal uncle, Stefano Rebaudi, and his wife Geronima acting as his godparents. Father Giovanni Nicora celebrated the sacrament. Little is known of Orengo's early life, though the Orengo name is of significant Ligurian lineage and can be traced back to the French region of Provence.[1] Notable Orengos include Marcantonio Orengo, a seventeenth-century philosopher, doctor, and author of a work on the treatment of plague victims; Paolo Girolamo Orengo, a Piarist priest elected bishop of Ventimiglia in 1804 and awarded the knight's cross of the Legion of Honor by Napoleon; Admiral Paolo Girolamo Orengo of the Italian Navy, born in 1828, knight of the Military Order of Italy and later an Italian senator; and Lorenzo Orengo (1838–1909), believed to be Fr. Orengo's young cousin, a leading sculptor of the brief artistic period known as Bourgeois Realism or naturalism in the 1860s and 1870s. The sculpture of this period elevated the values of work, progress, family, charity, and religion.[2] Lorenzo Orengo is famous for one monument, in particular, "La Venditrice di Noccioline" ("The Hazelnut Vendor") in the Monumental Cemetery of Staglieno in Genoa.

Around the age of sixteen or seventeen, Orengo entered the Dominicans, also known as the Order of Preachers, in the city of Viterbo in the Province of Rome. He took the religious name of Aloysius and would from that point forward be known as Luigi (Louis, in English), both a nickname for Aloysius and the name of his father.

Orengo took his habit at the historic Basilica of Santa Sabina, the mother church of the Order of Preachers. It's a building that dates to the third century and is well known for its cypress wood doors carved in AD 430–432 with biblical scenes, including the first-known publicly displayed depiction of the crucifixion of Jesus Christ and the two thieves.[3] Orengo made his profession of faith on March 11, 1838, and for the next three years studied at Santa Maria sopra Minerva in Rome. In 1841 he was assigned to the Priory of Saint Romanus in Lucca, where he studied for two years and likely received his priesthood. Records from both Minerva and Lucca "show him to have a good mind, and to have been a serious student."[4] It is during this period that Orengo likely met Bishop Richard Pius Miles, the prelate of the young Diocese of Nashville, which had been established only four years earlier in 1837. When Miles took possession of Nashville, after years of the area being served by the occasional missionary priest from Kentucky, there was only one rundown church, Holy Rosary Cathedral on what is now Capitol Hill, no resident priests, and about 130 Catholics. Relatively few of them would receive communion when given the chance.[5] In the entire state, only a few towns were visited by missionaries, and even then, at long intervals. The years had taken their toll.

"Through this isolation and neglect, the Catholics became scattered like sheep without a pastor," wrote Fr. Victor F. O'Daniel, OP, in his history of Miles, *The Father of the Church in Tennessee*. "Some

FIGURE 1.1. An undated photo of a young Fr. Louis Orengo.

of them left the state in order to find spiritual nourishment for their souls elsewhere. Others had grown weak in their faith or even lost it."[6]

Miles visited Rome in 1841 as part of a visit to France, Austria, and Italy to garner support and raise money for a seminary in Nashville. He had approximately three hundred Catholics in his diocese by then and needed more priests. The bishop's impassioned pleas in Rome may have worked on Orengo and inspired in him the desire to serve in the American missions.[7]

There were other visitors to Rome at this time—in addition to another visit by Miles in 1844—who may have put the idea in Orengo's mind. In November of 1842, George Augustine Joseph Wilson visited. An ex-carpenter and former Methodist from the Appalachian highlands of Western Virginia, Wilson was appointed to the post of Prior Provincial of St. Joseph's Province in Somerset, Ohio, by Dominican Master General Angelo Ancarani. He immediately planned a trip to Europe to recruit friars for the missions in America. He spent his first few months in the northeast United States trying to raise money for his trip, and in 1843 he proceeded to Rome to visit the General Chapter of the Dominicans. It is there that he met with Dominican friars Langdon Thomas Grace and Nicholas Raymond Young, American priests who were studying in Rome. He also met Orengo and fellow student priests Januaris Mannes (Gennaro) D'Arco and Sadoc Vilarrasa. The latter would go on to found the Province of the Holy Name in California.

The biggest influence on Orengo may have been a fellow Dominican in Rome. According to Fr. Paul-Marie Girardin, OP, who acted as Orengo's nurse for five years before his death, it was the legendary French priest Henri Lacordaire who encouraged Orengo's missions in America. In a letter from Fr. Girardin, then Chaplain of the Dominicans of Marino at the Monastero del SS. Rosario, to Fr. Victor O'Daniel in 1926, Girardin says that "(Orengo's) faculties were intact (and his) memory in particular was remarkable. He talked willingly about his missions in America. He often told me that he got his vocation as a missionary from Father Lacordaire, whom he had known very well in Rome when he was still a young student. 'Don't stay in Italy,' Father Lacordaire told him. 'Take care of the missions. The United States of America currently offers a field of action that opens up without limits for anyone who wants to give it their all.'"[8]

Lacordaire, already well known for his sermons in France, sought to rebuild the Catholic Church that the French Revolution had nearly decimated more than fifty years earlier. He believed a restoration of religious orders, especially the Dominicans with their focus on education and preaching, were his best means of doing this. He was ordained a Dominican in Rome in 1838 and returned to Paris in 1840 to reestablish the order there. He was Prior Provincial of the Dominicans in France from 1850 to 1854, and was largely responsible for the order's ascendancy as a significant religious and education force in the country.[9]

In 1844, something arrived in Italy that perhaps provided one more influence: a memoir by an Italian Dominican missionary who'd already been to America. Born and raised in Milan, Fr. Samuel Mazzuchelli also took his habit at Santa Sabina and was inspired by the visit of a high-ranking American clergyman to Rome: Edward Fenwick, the first Bishop of Cincinnati. Mazzuchelli immigrated to the United States in 1828 at the age of twenty-two. He traveled on horseback, foot, and canoe through Wisconsin and the Great Lakes area, serving Catholics, converting non-Catholics, establishing local parishes, and building more than two dozen churches and civic buildings on what was then the northwest frontier. On visits back to his native Italy in 1843 and 1844, midway through his missionary career, he wrote and published his memoirs. He gave them the lengthy title *Memoirs, Historical and Edifying, of a Missionary Apostolic of the Order of Preachers among Various Indian Tribes and among the Catholics and Protestants in the United States of America*. Mazzuchelli's stated intention for writing down his memoirs, which he did in the third person, was first and foremost for his fellow Dominicans. He wanted "to satisfy the eager wish of a number of devout persons, including the religious of the renowned Order of Preachers to which the missionary has the honor of belonging. These persons have shown an intense desire to learn about his labors in a region known in Europe, where, thanks to divine assistance, he was able to establish Catholic worship for the first time."[10]

He considered his second reason "of great weight:" to add to the ecclesiastical record of the United States of America and illuminate the obstacles and challenges of establishing the young dioceses of Detroit, Milwaukee, and Dubuque.

Ultimately, he added, "it is hoped that this little work, which may

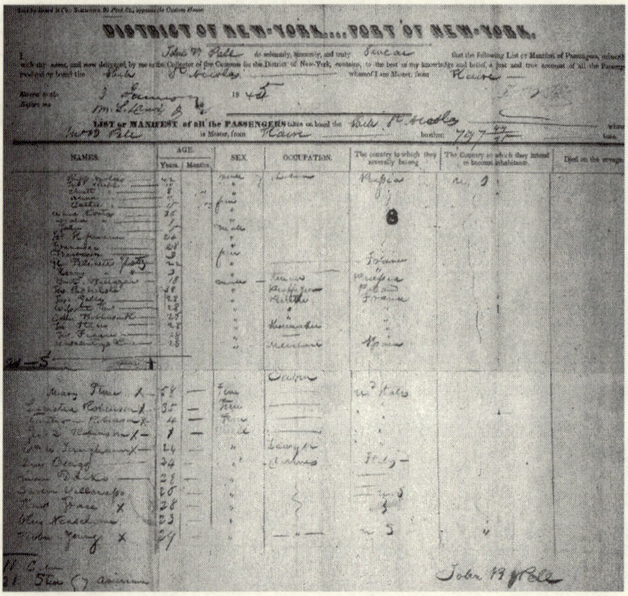

FIGURE 1.2. Ship manifest for the passenger ship *St. Nicolas*, which arrived in New York from Le Havre, France, on January 3, 1845. Aboard the ship were Frs. Louis Orengo, Thomas Grace, Raymond Young, Mannes D'Arco, and Sadoc Vilarrasa.

inspire some readers and strongly rouse the zeal of others for the propagation of the faith."

There is no specific evidence that Orengo and his fellow friars read Mazzuchelli's memoirs. But it's certain they knew of him and had heard of the book. The priest's missions in the United States were legendary and likely inspired the young priests to make their own mark on the burgeoning country.

On October 17, 1844, Orengo received his degree of Dominican Lector in Sacred Theology in Rome, and together with Grace, Young, D'Arco, and Vilarrasa, began his journey to the United States. Led by St. Joseph's Prior Provincial Wilson, they first traveled from Rome to the port of Le Havre, France. Le Havre was a key port of departure to the United States for many Europeans—and missionaries—in the nineteenth century. Mazzuchelli left for the United States from the port in 1822. Years later in 1889, another Italian who would make a significant impact on Catholicism in America, Frances Xavier (Mother) Cabrini, embarked from the same port.[11]

Wilson saw Orengo and his companions off from Le Havre on November 17, 1844, on the ship *St. Nicolas.*[12] Wilson then headed to Paris to continue his fundraising and recruitment work.

The passage to America seems to have gone smoothly. Vilarrasa gave a brief account of the journey to his family in a letter written from America: "After forty-eight days of sailing and without having encountered any danger, we landed in New York, thank God."[13]

According to his letter, the crew of Dominican friars disembarked in the afternoon of January 3, 1845, in New York City and immediately took a train to Philadelphia. On January 6, they left Philadelphia and traveled by train to Baltimore, where they remained overnight. The following day, they traveled yet again by rail about three hundred miles to a city—"the name of which" Vilarrasa could not remember—before making the final leg of their journey by stagecoach to St. Joseph's Province in Somerset, Perry County, Ohio. They arrived on January 9, 1845.

In 1845, the ministry of the friars of St. Joseph's Province was focused on the spiritual and pastoral. They preached the Gospel and cared for the poor. They gathered settlers for worship, built churches, and established parishes. Until 1850, they worked out of both St. Joseph's Priory in Somerset, Ohio and St. Rose Priory in Springfield, Kentucky. Friars were called from one or the other as required. From St. Joseph's they served missions at Lancaster and Zanesville, Ohio, as well as Holy Trinity Church in Somerset. They also visited outlying stations. Those stationed at St. Rose served St. Dominic's Church in Springfield, Holy Rosary Church in Manton, Kentucky, and nearby St. Magdalen's convent, the first congregation of Dominican Sisters in the county.

Upon arriving at St. Joseph's, Vilarrasa was almost immediately appointed novice master. D'Arco and Young stayed in Ohio to work among the people. Orengo and Grace were assigned to St. Rose.

St. Rose Priory, named in honor of the Third Order Dominican Saint Rose of Lima, was established in 1806 as the first Dominican religious house in the country. Its Tudor-Gothic church was built the same year, and to this day is the oldest standing structure west of the Allegheny Mountains still in use as a church.[14] Fr. Samuel Thomas Wilson, OP, was the church's first pastor. The Dominicans also established Saint Thomas College, a preparatory school for boys and young men, in 1808. It was the first Catholic educational institution west of the mountains. Among its notable alumni were Nashville Bishop Richard Pius Miles and Jefferson Davis, the president of the Confederacy during the Civil War.

Newly assigned to St. Rose, Orengo began to study English to prepare for missions. Grace worked in the parish.

Around the same time as Orengo's arrival in Kentucky, Miles offered Wilson and St. Joseph's Province a new opportunity in the Nashville diocese: The Church of St. Peter and St. Paul in Memphis. Established in 1840 by Fr. Michael McAleer, it was a parish with great lay support and a thriving congregation in a burgeoning city on the Mississippi River. While the population of Memphis in 1840 was only about 1,800, an influx of Irish and German immigrants and American migrants looking for work was quickly contributing to its growth. Eugene Magevney, an Irish immigrant from County Fermanagh whose home was the location of the first mass in Memphis two years earlier, helped found the parish.[15] Miles judged St. Peter's (as it came to be abridged and known) to be the best parish in his diocese. It certainly was, even if at the time there weren't many parishes to compare it to. Wilson was open to the invitation. It would be the province's first new mission since the death of Bishop Edward Fenwick in 1832 and play an important role in the life of both Orengo and the Catholic Church in Tennessee. While plans to take possession of the parish were worked out, Frs. Samuel Louis Montgomery and Joseph Alemany, who had been assigned to St. Joseph's Province since 1841 and had already conducted missions in Tennessee, were assigned to Tennessee to help Miles in Memphis and elsewhere.

By 1846, Orengo was preaching at Saint Dominic's in Springfield, Kentucky, a young church built in January 1844 on Armory Hill in what was then considered south of town. A frame building painted white and about 55' × 25' in size, it was at St. Dominic's that the first bit of mythology around Orengo's indefatigable and boundless energy began to materialize.[16]

As research for his 1926 book on Miles, Fr. Victor O'Daniel conducted numerous interviews with aging priests and parishioners who remembered Orengo. Thomas Simms was one. "He was quite athletic," Simms apparently told O'Daniel. "The first time or two he said mass there (at St. Dominic), not noticing that the stairway leading up to the pulpit was on the church side of the altar railing and that he had to leave the sanctuary to get to the stairway, he simply. . . leaped into the pulpit to give his sermon. After the sermon he leaped out of the pulpit into the sanctuary."[17] Fr. Eugene Gazzo, who Orengo mentored and later became the pastor of St. Peter's in Memphis, told O'Daniel that perhaps what happened in St. Dominic's was merely a prelude to the zeal that would eventually define Orengo. "[Orengo] was very quick and agile," Gazzo said in 1824. "He could clear any fence without the least difficulty [and] would frequently step over the altar railing than walk to the gate. He was tireless."[18]

When you are as full of energy as Orengo, being cloistered simply won't do, and on August 22, 1846, in a letter to Dominican Master General Vincenzo Ajello, Orengo complained that he came to America to do missionary work, "a work for which there is great need," but that Wilson had assigned him to St. Rose to live the life of a contemplative monk. Orengo appealed to the general to set him free to go on the missions, "to labor on the missions among the Indians, or negroes, or other unbelievers," since, he says, he can now speak not only English, but the dialect of Blacks as well. It's not inconceivable that with a basis in French, Italian, Latin, and now the English he was learning, Orengo conceived of himself as some kind of fluid master of linguistics. He was ready to hit the road.

In the opening months of 1848, Orengo finally got his wish and was sent to Nashville to help Miles. He traveled by horseback from Springfield, Kentucky to Nashville, about a 175-mile journey, and arrived shortly after Miles had returned from a visit to West Tennessee, where the bishop had administered confirmation, on February 27, 1848, to twenty-four Catholics.[19]

Miles was delighted.

"Hardly had the bishop reached home when he was rejoiced by the arrival of an Italian priest who soon proved one of the most zealous and self-sacrificing missionaries of Tennessee," wrote O'Daniel in his biography of Miles.

Miles wasted no time in putting Orengo to work. March 26, 1848, is the date of the first recorded baptism performed by the priest in Nashville in the newly completed cathedral in downtown Nashville, St. Mary of the Seven Sorrows.

A little over a month later, on May 2, 1848, Fr. Joseph Alemany was appointed Prior Provincial of St. Joseph's. Alemany's missionary experience in Tennessee meant the prior knew what was needed in the state. Those experiences modified previous views he might have had on study and strict monastic observance. He once believed that long intensive study of theology was necessary on the frontier. If mission needs conflicted with the requirements of observance, the new provincial would give priority to the good of the Church.[20]

Toward the end of his first year in the diocese, Orengo received a letter from Alemany. "It is true that you might be very useful in Ohio

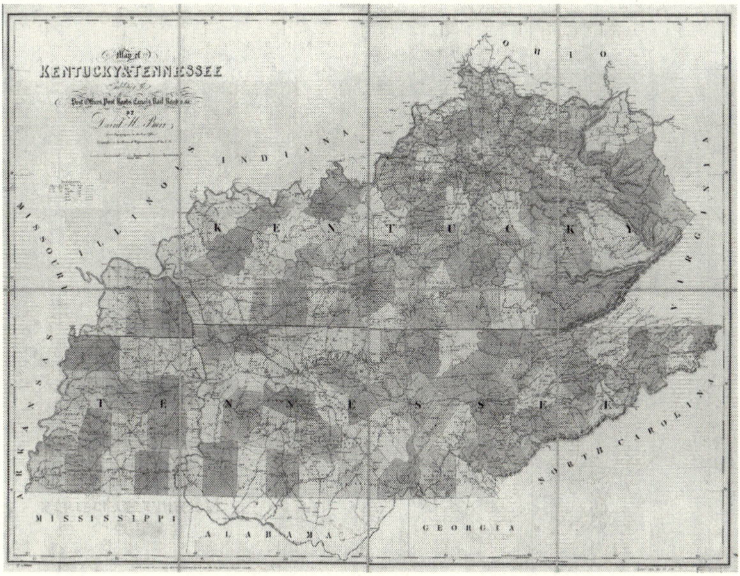

FIGURE 1.3. "Map of Kentucky and Tennessee exhibiting the post offices, post roads, canals, rail roads, &c.; by David. H. Burr (Late topographer to the Post Office) Geographer to the House of Representatives of the U.S." London, 1839. Library of Congress, Geography and Map Division.

or other places," wrote the prior, "but on the other hand I think that Bp. Miles deserves far greater help than what we give him."

The stage was set for Orengo in Tennessee. His first mission was to be assigned resident priest of St. Mary's Church in Clarksville. From Clarksville, Orengo could venture out on horseback to both struggling and established missions throughout Middle and West Tennessee, ministering to the scattered Catholics along the way. In Humphreys County, on a trip to Memphis from Nashville, Orengo met a community of mostly Irish Catholic immigrant laborers in what is now known as McEwen. It is where he'd establish his greatest legacy.

CHAPTER 2

The Tennessee Missions

In 1844, Nashville Bishop Richard Pius Miles purchased land in Clarksville, Montgomery County, Tennessee on Washington Street (now College Street) between 4th and 5th Streets. Located in northwest Middle Tennessee on the Cumberland River, close to the border with Kentucky, Clarksville was at this time already an important farming, trade, and transportation hub. Its Highland Rim soil produced sought-after dark-fired tobacco, a flavorful and dark tobacco often used in cigar, pipe, and chewing tobacco. Thanks to the arrival of the steamboat in 1820, which turned the Cumberland River and its connected waterways into bustling river highways, dark-fired tobacco was shipped internationally via ports in New Orleans and Pittsburgh on the Mississippi River. The fertile soil and promise of work attracted Irish Catholic settlers to the area who needed missionary priests to serve them.[1]

Fr. Ivo Schacht, known as the "Builder of the Church in Tennessee," laid the cornerstone for a church that June. Six months later in December of 1844, a 20' × 40' brick building was dedicated as Saint Mary Catholic Church. While St. Mary's brought the potential of stability to the Catholics in Clarksville, finding priests to consistently minister to them was a constant challenge for Miles. When Orengo arrived in Tennessee in 1848, Clarksville was where Miles sent him. It would be his base until 1855, and the location from which he'd be

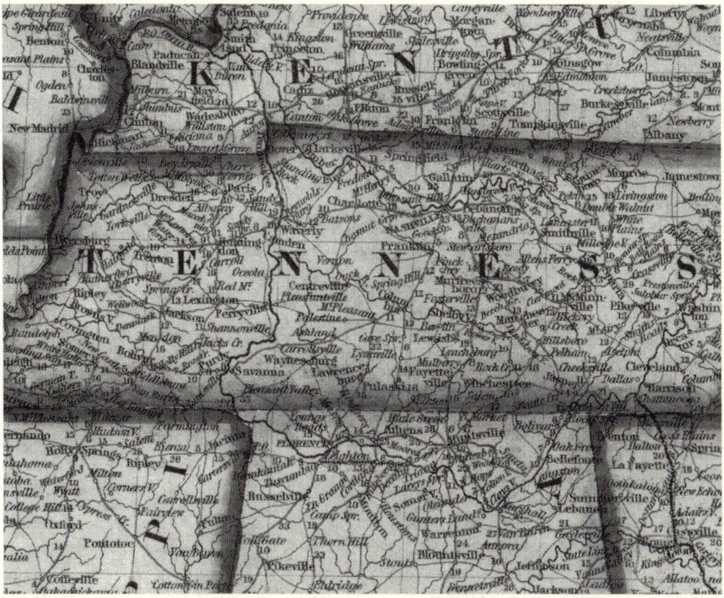

FIGURE 2.1. Detail of a map of Tennessee stage roads with distances, published by Sherman & Smith in 1850. Library of Congress, Geography and Map Division.

able to serve the faithful in Montgomery County and the Catholics scattered about in missions throughout West Tennessee.

Orengo likely traveled to Clarksville by horseback on the stagecoach road. Up until the beginning of the Civil War in 1861, there were sixteen major stagecoach lines departing from Nashville, using four horse teams, and carrying as many as fifteen passengers. Departing from Nashville they ran to Louisville, Chattanooga, Memphis (including stops in Charlotte, Reynoldsburg, Huntingdon, Jackson, Bolivar, Sommerville, and Raleigh), Huntsville, Tuscumbia, Florence, Clarksville, Hopkinsville, Springfield, and Russellville.[2] Smaller accommodation coaches ran to Triune, Nolensville, Gallatin, Lebanon, and Columbia.[3] By 1850, the Southwestern Stage depot in Nashville was "the closest thing to Grand Central Station Tennessee had at the time" according to historian Bill Carey.[4] The stagecoach line that ran through the Humphreys County area, approximately one-half mile north of present-day McEwen, existed as early as 1812.[5] As it was "ideally situated" between New Orleans and Washington, it is believed that many important people crossed through this area on the stagecoach line, including Andrew Jackson and his volunteer army on his way from the Hermitage to fight the Battle of New Orleans.[6]

Orengo wasn't the first priest to arrive in Humphreys County. Like in Clarksville, Fr. Schacht beat him to it by a few years, dispatched by Miles to build a small church for the Irish Catholic laborers who had settled there and started families. How they got there has to do with two devout Catholics, Dr. Federick Hopkins Knapp, a dentist from New Orleans, and his brother-in-law, James F. Neale, who purchased five thousand acres for a sheep farm in present-day McEwen in a bankruptcy sale in 1842. Knapp brought with him more than two dozen Irish immigrants, considered the poorest of the poor.[7] Among their surnames were McEnroe, McGuire, Devoy, Murphee, May, Hennissy, Sheen, Faherity, and Taylor. Others who settled in the area at Knapp and Neale's urging were the Sheehy, Murphy, Sheehan, Hinson, and O'Flaherty families.[8] A Catholic community was formed. Miles took notice and began sending missionary priests to visit the area every couple of months. "This is a new plantation comprising a large tract of good and cheap land," Miles is quoted as writing, "sixty miles from Nashville near the Tennessee River and on the stage road from Nashville to Memphis."[9] Knapp eventually donated one thousand acres of his property to Miles and the diocese to begin "a church for the workers."[10] As part of the donation, Knapp asked that some of the land be sold at a rate of twenty-five cents per acre "to attract more Catholic families to settle in the area."[11]

Fr. Schacht began serving the community between 1844 and 1846 and started construction on its first church, a log chapel located on the road between present-day McEwen and White Oak.[12] This church was dedicated by Schact on Easter Sunday, March 23, 1845.[13]

By the following year, the church was known as St. Patrick's, possibly because of the significant Irish population in the area.

It was this community and church that Fr. Orengo encountered when he first visited the area in 1849, on his way to Memphis from Nashville. The Italian priest appears to have been almost immediately taken with this Irish community, at the time being attended to once a month by Fr. Louis Hoste from Nashville.[14] Orengo purchased one hundred acres from John Massey for a farm at the head of Trace Creek and began offering mass in private homes, possibly because the original log church built by Schacht was either in disrepair or simply no longer sufficed. He soon erected a new small log church where the original Schacht structure stood and began expanding the community with an encouraging pitch. "Seeing how hard it was for people with young families to live by their daily labor in towns, and meet the expenses thereof," wrote St. Patrick's parishioner Eliza Pyburn in a St. Patrick's Parish history in 1909, "[Orengo] induced several to leave Nashville, Clarksville and other places, and buy the land then cheap, of Humphreys County, where they and their children could live by cultivating the soil." Those other places included nearby Dickson, Houston, and Stewart Counties, all part of the West Iron Belt, a rich North/South swath of brown iron ore deposits in the Western Highland Rim of Tennessee. Irish immigrants were working in numerous blast furnaces in the area, which chemically reduced large amounts of ore and limestone flux into molten metal and waste material.[15] Orengo was already ministering to these immigrants in his travels. It's clear he had won their trust.

St. Patrick's, which sat near the western edge of Middle Tennessee, was visited by Orengo on horseback the second Sunday of every other month in 1849.[16] He also attended St. Mary's in Clarksville the first Sunday of every month and the second Sunday every other month (leapfrogging with St. Patrick's); the mission in Murfreesboro, southwest of Nashville in Rutherford County, the fourth Sunday of every other month; Franklin in Williamson County every third Sunday; Columbia the fourth Sunday of every other month (presumably alternating with Murfreesboro); and Shelbyville in Bedford County and Dover in Stewart County once a month. It's enough to make your head spin. Shelbyville, in southwest Middle Tennessee, and Dover, in northwest Middle Tennessee, are at least 125 miles from each other as the crow flies.

There are secondary sources that indicate Orengo also visited Jackson, Tennessee, halfway between Nashville and Memphis, at this time, even suggesting that he built a church in 1849.[17] There's no record of him being there at this time, however. And while *The Catholic Almanacs* from 1848 to 1850 do list a mission in Jackson attended to by priests from St. Peter's in Memphis, they do not mention a church. Jackson would figure in Orengo's Tennessee ministry eventually, but not for another decade or so.

In 1850, a document was issued by the Dominicans that would have a major effect on St. Joseph's Province and further embed Orengo in Tennessee. One of Orengo's great supporters, Fr. Joseph Alemany, St. Joseph's Prior Provincial, was named the new Bishop of the Diocese of Monterey, California. Additionally, the document stated that "Father Orengo is to remain with Bishop Miles as long as the bishop lives."[18] It must have a been a welcome declaration for Miles, who by 1850 estimated 3,000 Catholics in Tennessee, up from 1,500 in 1948. He needed every priest he could find, especially one with Orengo's energy.

With Orengo's immediate future more clearly defined, Miles continued to make the most of his zealous Dominican. In 1850, Orengo is not only listed in the clergy in Nashville, where according to the *Nashville Union* newspaper he had a letter waiting for him at the post office, he kept up a somewhat similar schedule to the previous year.[19] He continued to celebrate mass for the faithful in Clarksville the first Sunday of every month, was at St. Patrick's in Humphreys County the second Sunday of every other month, and in Murfreesboro the fourth Sunday of the month. In the latter half of the year, he also appears in West Tennessee, helping his friend and former St. Rose Priory roommate Fr. Thomas Grace at St. Peter's in Memphis. His first entry in the baptism registry at St. Peter's is July 8, 1850. He continued this schedule in 1851, and in 1852, added Dover (again) and Gallatin to his rounds.

In Gallatin, there is a diocesan record on March 4, 1853, of Orengo baptizing a six-month-old enslaved girl, Isabella, belonging to Francis Rogan. According to Orengo's notes accompanying the record, she appears to be the daughter of an enslaved woman named Puss. "Her stepmother," writes Orengo, indicating the child's godmother in baptism, "was Martha Rogan."[20] Martha was Francis's wife and the granddaughter of notable Tennessee pioneer and settler Isaac Bledsoe.

Orengo's baptism of an enslaved girl is one of the few records connecting him with the institution of slavery in Tennessee. This may have to do with the fact that the poor communities he served were made up mostly of Irish immigrant laborers who did not own slaves. In at least one instance, as relayed by Emma Grisham in *A Folk History of Slavery in the United States From Interviews with Former Slaves*, it seems that sometimes during the Civil War those Irish immigrants were hired to work on plantations alongside the enslaved to keep an eye on things, but only when fighting got severe and white slaveholders no longer felt safe.[21] In the eyes of white slaveowners, the Irish were barely a step up from enslaved African Americans (and in some ways, not being property, more expendable). It explains why many Irish Catholics might have opposed the Union cause, supported the Confederacy, and opposed abolition. It was hard enough finding work without having to compete with freed Black men, who were already being brought in to break strikes and getting paid even less than the Irish. When in March of 1863 Congress nationalized conscription into the Federal Army, Irish Catholics in New York City started burning down draft offices and blocking trains with draftees. The casualties at Antietam and Fredericksburg further enflamed them, and by July of that year, New York had descended into a full-scale riot. Police superintendent John Kennedy was beaten to near-death, an orphanage for Black children was burned down, and thousands of Black residents were forced to flee the city. Federal troops were pulled from Gettysburg to maintain order. Irish Catholic immigrants, poor and destitute, were simply not having it. Maintaining the status quo of slavery at least gave them a modicum of a chance. That reality, while offering no clue as to whether Orengo had a moral opposition to slavery, helps inform what might have at least been his complicated economic opposition to it.[22] It made it hard for poor Catholic immigrants and laborers to find work (unless you needed them to protect your plantation). Its abolition would have only made it harder. As Orengo would write to a former parishioner in Humboldt, Tennessee, years later, "Except Memphis and Nashville other places in Tennessee offer poor encouragement for Catholics. The negros are the laborers there." For Orengo, "Catholics" and "laborers" were the same thing. Encouragement equated to opportunities—to make an honest living, provide for your family, and build a life. The work the poor Catholics were able to do, outside of skilled stone mason labor in the city, was done by enslaved workers. Why would those who owned slaves hire poor Irish immigrants?

As far as Irish Catholics go, Francis and Martha Rogan were an anomaly. They were neither immigrants nor laborers. They were second-generation Irish Americans and relatively wealthy landowners firmly ensconced in the agrarian way of life in the America South. They were also descendants of one of Tennessee's founding Catholic families. Francis, fifty-five years old when Isabella was baptized, was the youngest son of Hugh Rogan, who is credited with establishing the Catholic Church in Sumner County, Tennessee, where Gallatin is located, in the late 1700s. Hugh Rogan arrived in the United States from County Donegal, Ireland, in the spring of 1775, in the Port of Philadelphia, on one of the last ships to land before the American Revolution began. In Ireland, Hugh Rogan was a member of the "Irish Defenders," a group of Catholic agrarian reformers resisting the minority Protestant rule over the Catholic majority. His decision to immigrate to the American colonies, leaving behind his wife, Nancy, and infant son, Bernard, may have been the result of his role in the Defenders. In the late 1770s, he got a job, along with Isaac Bledsoe, supporting the Continental Army as a guard with the party who surveyed and marked the boundaries of North Carolina and Virginia. He then returned to what is now the Nashville area as a member of the John Donelson party, which traveled by river to meet James Robertson's overland group at Fort Nashborough in 1780. He was one of 250 men who signed the Cumberland Compact, a document that outlined how the settlers at Fort Nashborough and the six other forts that made up the Cumberland settlement would govern themselves.[23] Over the next two decades, he became a defender of the area's settlements and a legendary fighter against the Indians. For his service to the Continental Army, Hugh Rogan was originally granted land both near the present location of Vanderbilt University and in Sumner County but traded the former to combine it with the latter, creating a farm that totaled almost one thousand acres. He went back to Ireland—almost twenty years after leaving—to retrieve his wife and son. Together they built "Rogana," a two-room stone house patterned after an Irish folk cottage. It was there in 1798 that Francis was born.

Devout Catholics who experienced persecution in Ireland, the Rogans were determined to continue to practice their faith. Even without an attending priest, Rogana became the center of Catholic

FIGURE 2.2. Rogana as it stands today at Bledsoe's Fort Historical Park in Sumner County, Tennessee. Photo courtesy of the author.

life in Sumner County. Those assembled at the home celebrated "missa sicca"—dry masses—which are essentially shortened versions of the mass that omit the offertory, consecration, and communion. It is believed that by the time of his death in 1813, Hugh hadn't seen a priest in more than fifty years. His son, Francis, didn't see a priest until he was thirty years old. Yet somehow, they sustained their faith. Bernard, the son Hugh retrieved when he returned to Ireland, first moved to the area now known as Missouri and served in the War of 1812. Bernard returned to Sumner County in 1828. Upon his death in 1873, just shy of his one hundredth birthday, the *Nashville Union and American* noted, "Throughout life he was always true to the cause and the religion of Ireland, preserving his faith in these western wilds for half a century without seeing priest or church, a Roman Catholic and an uncompromising States-rights Democrat."[24]

In 1998, Rogana was dismantled, moved, and reconstructed a few miles away at Bledsoe's Fort Historical Park, where it can be viewed today and occasionally toured. It is surrounded by interpretative panels that tell the story of Hugh Rogan and the early Catholic community there. A headstone-like monument honoring Hugh Rogan as a "Revolutionary War Patriot" was placed adjacent to Rogana by the General Jethro Sumner Chapter of the Daughters of the American Revolution in 2017. To visit the house today, touch its stones and peer into its windows, is a pilgrimatic experience. The building predates both the long-gone Holy Rosary Cathedral established on Capitol Hill (then Cedar Knob) in the 1820s, and the home of French Canadian, Catholic statesman, fur-trapper, and "Nashville's First Citizen," Timothy Demonbreun, on 3rd Avenue in downtown Nashville, where it's believed the first mass celebrated by a bishop was held in 1821.[25] Rogana stands as Middle Tennessee's earliest physical connection to Catholicism in the region, and a place Orengo certainly visited and likely celebrated mass in the mid-nineteenth century.

CHAPTER 3

Many Hardships

> They strengthened the spirits of the disciples and exhorted them to persevere in the faith, saying, "It is necessary for us to undergo many hardships to enter the kingdom of God."
>
> —Acts 14:22, New American Bible, rev. ed.

Established roads notwithstanding, the West Tennessee territory that Orengo was venturing into in the mid-nineteenth century was still dangerous, especially as we'll see, for a lone Catholic priest on horseback. St. Patrick's parishioner John Lehman thought the danger significant enough that he included it in a history he wrote about Orengo and the parish that was published abridged in the Catholic newspaper *The Tennessee Register* on Sunday, May 15, 1949, to commemorate the Centenary of St. Patrick's Church in McEwen. The published article was headlined "McEwen Parish to Commemorate Centenary on May 29, 1949."[1] In a letter dated eighteen years later, on February 10, 1967, written to Fr. George Flanigen, founding editor of *The Register* and author of *Catholicity in Tennessee: A Sketch of Catholic Activities in the State, 1541–1937*, Lehman said some of the original article he had written was left out of the published version. "You may publish this again at your convenience if you wish," wrote Lehman, before noting some of the original settlers of McEwen who were left out of the article.

He closed his letter: "Father, I am in my 91st year. Please remember me in your prayers. Thanks, yours in Christ. John Lehman."[2]

Lehman, nearing the end of his days, clearly thought his history was worth a second look.

Wild West Tennessee

The history submitted to *The Register* was originally titled by Lehman, "Father Orengo—One of the First Priests in McEwen." Lehman began his history with a story well known to those in Humphreys County: the murder in August 1842 of Fulton, Arkansas, businessman William Kopman on the old stage road between Memphis and Nashville, fourteen miles east of Waverly. A *Nashville American* article in 1905 called it "one of the most brutal murders ever recorded in the annals of our state."[3] The writer of the article, C. B. Hardwood, recalls traveling the old stage road as a young man in 1857:

> I was quite a lad at that time, and I remember well after passing Waverly on our way to Nashville as we were crossing what was then call Seven-mile Ridge, where not a house was to be seen, when we reached a point about one-third of the way across the buggies all stopped, and all parties got out, and we were told that this was the spot where a man by the name of Kopman had been murdered. We were shown the grave where he was buried, although fifteen years had elapsed since the murder yet we could see the rails and puncheons which had been used as seats when the funeral of the murdered man had been preached. It made quite an impression on my young mind.[4]

An account of the murder was reported in the *Nashville Union* on September 9, 1842. The basic facts of the story as reported by the paper are that Kopman, a partner in the Fulton, Arkansas, firm of

Haywood & Kopman, had business in Winchester, Tennessee. Kopman packed several thousand dollars for the trip, mostly gold, in his saddlebags. He stayed in both Memphis and Huntingdon, where he apparently had friends or family. Leaving Huntingdon, he crossed the Tennessee River via the Reynoldsburg Ferry. When he got to Waverly, he stayed at the hostelry owned by Spencer T. Hunt. While there, he noticed in the register that Joseph Stalcop of Washington, Arkansas, a man he was acquainted with, had stayed there the night before. The next morning after breakfast, Kopman continued his journey. Two days later, near present-day McEwen, Kopman's body, covered with brush, was found with a bullet hole in his head. Four hundred yards away, his saddle, saddlebags, bridle, and hat were found. His horse, without bridle or saddle, had somehow made it back to Hunt's hostelry.

Both Hunt and Stalcop were arrested for the murder, but both were acquitted for lack of evidence. Not long after the acquittal, another person, "an indolent and worthless man by the name of Etheridge" according to the *Union*, was found in possession of a $20 gold piece. He claimed he received the money for burying Kopman's body but refused to divulge the name of whom he got it from. He was tried and convicted for the murder, and sentenced to life in prison, where he died.

What does any of this have to do with Orengo? Well, nothing and everything. Nothing because Lehman has his dates incorrect. He has Orengo arriving in Humphreys County only days before Kopman (Lehman refers to him as Kauffman) was murdered. "A few nights before [Kopman's murder] Father Orengo traveled on a large Black Horse like unto the one Kauffman rode," wrote Lehman. "Was held up at almost the same spot Kauffman was murdered. No doubt the robbers upon questioning him were convinced he wasn't the one they were seeking. Therefore let him go on his way from that time on."

Orengo didn't arrive in Humphreys County until six years after Kopman's murder. It has everything to do with Orengo because of the context it provides for the West Tennessee world Orengo was entering in 1848, a place still very much the frontier, and how his arrival is remembered. Lehman was born in 1876, a full generation after the murder and the arrival of Orengo. He surely grew up hearing about both events, which by the time he was a young adult had become local legends. He can be forgiven for conflating the two: the story of "one of the most brutal murders ever recorded in the annals of our state" with the arrival of a hero priest on a black horse who evades would-be robbers to arrive in the area and lift the community up out of a dark history.

The threat of robbers was only one of many hardships Orengo faced during his first years in Middle Tennessee, as he traversed the area southeast from Clarksville to Nashville and then west to Humphreys County; southeast to Murfreesboro and then north to Dover and south to Franklin and beyond, "trying to introduce a semblance of sacramental regularity into the people's lives."[5] St. Patrick's parishioner Eliza Pyburn, in a 1909 history of the parish, elaborates:

> In the early years of his ministry in Humphreys County, Father Orengo suffered untold hardships, living in a log house near the church alone, doing his own cooking—a meal very often consisted of a piece of corn bread and a slice of fat bacon; his lunch the same, which he often carried many miles through the woods while traveling to church in distant parts of the county. His only means of travel was on horseback; and when tired and hungry (he) would stop for a while by the roadside and rest, partake of his dainty lunch. He was met with many unpleasant incidents; and his life was one of toil and hardship, but he never complained, being satisfied to be able to minister to the wants of his parish

> and brings souls to God; which he did through many conversions among the people with whom he mingled, and whose descendants are today the strictest members of his old parish.[6]

"Few priests nowadays in Tenn. have any idea of the hardships, trials and tribulations that poor Fr. Orengo had to suffer from the torrid heat of the summer and frigid cold of winter," wrote Patrick Quinan in his intriguing 1909 history of Orengo. Quinan was asked by Fr. Edward J. Kuettner of Humboldt, Tennessee, to write a short biography of Orengo for Fr. John K. Larkin of Johnson City, Tennessee, who was at the time collecting stories for a history of the church in Tennessee. The letter from Kuettner to Larkin included with Quinan's history is interesting (and somewhat sadly humorous) in how explicit Kuettner is in disparaging the amateur historian's work. Writes Kuettner, "The writer has been dilatory in undertaking to write a short biographical sketch of the Rev. Louis (Aloysius) Orengo, one of the greatest missionary priests that ever officiated in the diocese of Nashville, Tenn., because he is utterly incompetent to do justice to the memory of a priest who possessed the religious zeal, piety, and learning he did."

Even though he didn't appreciate the work, Kuettner still sent the sketch along to Larkin. Quinan's dates are questionable, and he tends to digress from his topic, but there are still some interesting anecdotes in it to consider.

> [Orengo] was often landed at midnight on the banks of the Tenn. or Cumberland rivers, having to wait perhaps several hours, hungry and thirsty, for a boat or some mode of convenience to take him to the next camp or settlement. He sometimes rode mule back and very often "Shanks Mare," carrying his valise several miles on a cold frosty day. At the present time a priest can organize a

> dance, euchre party, or picnic and raise enough money to meet expenses, but he never makes any converts as did Fr. Orengo.[7]

That Quinan mentions a picnic as one of the things Orengo could not have done in his time means that in 1909, the fundraising event that Orengo created at St. Patrick's in McEwen in the mid-1850s, which was still going strong in 1909, must have been a relatively small affair in Humphreys County. It had yet to reach the people eighty miles west of McEwen in Humboldt, or the legendary status it has today as the World's Largest Barbecue and longest-running festival in Tennessee. But more on that in a bit.

For another look at the hardships that Orengo faced, we can look at an oral history provided by Fr. Eugene Titus Gazzo, OP, to Fr. Victor F. O'Daniel in 1924 as O'Daniel was researching his book on Bishop Miles. Born in 1848, Gazzo immigrated to the United States in 1871, getting to know his fellow countryman Orengo for at least two years before the latter ended his missions in Tennessee. O'Daniel spoke with Gazzo, then seventy-six years old, in October 1924, just about seven months before Gazzo's death on April 6, 1925. His anecdotes about Orengo are vivid and worth sharing as O'Daniel recorded them.

> On one occasion Father Orengo was stopped by a robber who wanted his horse. Father Orengo, who was not mounted on his own steed, replied: "Why this is the bishop's horse. You wouldn't want to take his Lordship's horse. He needs it too badly." The robber somewhat nonplused by Father Orengo's coolness, and perhaps also by the word "Lordship," asked: "What time is it?" Father Orengo, fearing to take out his watch lest the robber should demand it, looked at the sun in order to give an approximate answer to the question. The robber also looked up at the sky.

> Then Father Orengo, quickly as a flash, dashed into the bushes that grew in the woods that skirted the road, and escaped.
>
> He often, while on his journeys, slept in the woods, hitching his horse and using his saddle for a pillow. The saddle-blanket served as his covering. His food, at such times especially, was cheese and crackers, which he always carried in his pockets. He was nearly always on the road looking up negligent and fallen-away Catholics. Often, he rode horseback from Nashville to Memphis and back. Hardly would be rested, when he would start on a similar journey into east Tennessee, travelling as far as the boundary lines of Virginia and North Carolina. A journey that extended only through the width of the state from the Kentucky to the Georgia or Alabama line he considered short. He always made it a point to go by one route and to return by another; for this gave him a better opportunity to discover the kind of people for whom he was searching.
>
> He was tireless. Such was his zeal, and such his industry, that no labor in the cause of souls, the Church or charity seemed to fatigue him. No one could understand how could do with so little sleep, food or rest.[8]

The Nashville Daily American in 1882 has a similar retelling of Gazzo's story of Orengo evading robbers. He must have shared it often. It comes in an interview with Fr. Louis Hoste, who first came to Nashville in 1841 with Bishop Miles and stayed in the area until 1865. In 1882, he returned to visit the city and celebrate mass at the Cathedral of St. Mary of the Seven Sorrows on January 8. *The Daily American* took the opportunity to ask Hoste about his recollections of the city in the early days of the diocese, and in the process, shared with him the story about Orengo they had heard from Gazzo. There are slight variations. The newspaper reports Orengo referring to the bishop, not "his Lordship." It also appears the robbers had their eyes on Orengo's clothes, to which Orengo replies dismissively, "Rags!" After evading the thieves, Orengo apparently bought a compass and took the woods instead of the highways.

"Yes," responded Hoste to this anecdote. "Missionaries in those days were forced to take care of themselves in their long and lonesome rides."[9] Long journeys on horseback; sleeping under the stars; subsisting on modest rations; the threat of robbers. While all of these would have been hardships for Orengo and certainly make his work heroic, they would not have been that unique for any other kind of missionary at the time, or any other person who made their living traveling. Rural Tennessee in 1850 was still very much the frontier. What makes Orengo's accomplishments particularly extraordinary at this time is the additional threat he faced simply for being Catholic.

Fear of Catholics

There was no hiding who he was. In recollections provided by those who cared for Orengo in his final years, they recall him mentioning several times that did not wear the full Dominican habit while on horseback, but it's likely that he would have at least been wearing a black cassock as Fr. Samuel Mazzuchelli did in the Midwest decades earlier, taking a lead from Jesuit missionaries in the century prior.[10] Anti-Catholic vitriol at the time could result in extreme and unreasonable reactions by those who believed what they heard.

On one occasion in Orengo's travels, being tired and weary as the night descended, he remembered that he knew of an Irish Catholic man who lived a few miles away. He knew the man's wife wasn't Catholic, but thinking he would likely get a good night's lodging, he took a chance traveling to the house. "Vain were his hopes," writes Pyburn. The wife answered the door, and when Orengo announced himself, she went into the house and returned with a butcher knife: "He had to wander through the darkness of the night, and loneliness of the woods until he found (a place) at last to rest through what remained of the night."[11]

On another occasion, Orengo was asked to administer last rites to a man in Nashville who was dying. The man's wife, however, like the woman who chased him away with a butcher knife, was not Catholic—not of "the household of faith" as Pyburn writes it—and when she answered the door, she ordered him off and slammed the door in his face. The man died without last rites, leaving two sons who the mother raised Protestant.

These kinds of extreme responses to a Catholic priest showing up at your door were stoked by years of anti-Catholic rhetoric from both the Protestant press and pulpit. Much of it was already there and building before Orengo even arrived in Tennessee.

James Robinson Graves, the pastor of Central Baptist Church in Nashville, began editing the *Tennessee Baptist* in 1846, and nine years later, launched *The Southern Baptist Review and Eclectic*. He believed that the Catholic Church and all non-Baptist Protestant denominations were intent on overthrowing republican governments. He was particularly opposed to the Roman Catholic Church, which he referred to as "Romanism," and saw it only as a den of thieves and blood thirsty prosecutors. He believed the papacy's power depended "upon kidnapping and enslaving the infancy of humanity in its cradle." He proclaimed a crusade against what he called the "infant slave trade."[12] Nativists, "charged with the Protestant evangelical fervor of the day," wrote John Higham in his 1955 book, *Strangers in the Land: Patterns of American Nativism, 1860–1925*, "considered the immigrants minions of the Roman despot, dispatched here to subvert American institutions."[13]

Methodist preacher James L. Chapman took the criticism even

further in his 1856 book *Americanism vs. Romanism, or, The Cis-Atlantic Battle Between Sam & the Pope.* As he saw it, the Catholic Church had substituted a pope for an emperor, images of saints for heathen idols, crafty Jesuits for the Apostles, and the Inquisition for the temple of liberty: "Romanism cared not, heeded not, shed not a tear of regret over its bloodstained acts, damnable policies, and hellish inventions."[14]

The concept of individual freedom was embedded in the national culture. Nativists "were tempted to view American liberty and European popery as irreconcilable."[15] Considering these criticisms, it's hard to blame a non-Catholic woman for not wanting her infant child enslaved, or her fatherless sons beholden to an emperor in Italy.

The Know-Nothings

The anti-Catholic sentiment that Orengo encountered on his arrival in Middle Tennessee and West Tennessee was not only because of his faith, but also because of the faithful it attracted. Spurred in part by the horrors of the Great Potato Famine in Ireland in the second half of the 1840s and the promise of opportunity in America, immigration in the United States jumped from more than 128,000 in 1820 to almost three million in the 1850s. Between 1850 and 1860, a third of the population growth in the United States, from twenty-three million to thirty-one million was due to immigration. With the growth came visible poverty, a more vocal labor class, and an increase in crime. Immigration was an easy scapegoat.[16] While there was already a burgeoning nativist movement in the United States by middle- and upper-class citizens who claimed "American" ancestry, virulent anti-immigrant—and therefore anti-Catholic sentiment—reached new heights by the mid-1850s.

Enter the Know-Nothings.

It began with the Order of the Star-Spangled Banner, a secret oath-bound society formed in 1849 in New York to intimidate immigrants and discourage Catholicism.[17]

The Order of the Star-Spangled Banner gave birth to the American Party. To be a member, one had to be an American-born Protestant male without a Catholic wife or parents, and pledge to keep foreigners and Roman Catholics out of decent jobs and public office. If Catholics already held public office, members of the American Party pledged to remove them wherever legally possible. Because of the party's secrecy, members often replied "I know nothing" when asked about their dealings. Hence the name. In 1854, they began winning significant seats in local and state elections, and by the fall of the year, elected seventy-five men to Congress. In 1855, they also did well in many northern and southern state elections, including Tennessee.[18] Incumbent Tennessee governor Andrew Johnson, who while not Catholic was known to occasionally attend Catholic services and speak in defense of its practitioners, narrowly defeated Whig candidate Meredith Poindexter Gentry in that year's gubernatorial election by only 2,157 votes.[19] Gentry, in his campaign speeches, stuck close to the Know-Nothing platform, spewing plenty of anti-Catholic and xenophobic rhetoric. All of this was kindling for potential violence.

In November 1855, a mob of Know-Nothings surrounded the St. Xavier Convent of the Sisters of Mercy in Providence, Rhode Island, planning to burn it down. Local Irish immigrants positioned themselves within the walled convent garden, assuring Mother Superior Mary Frances Wade that "they would, by God's blessing, guard her and hers from evil."[20] The bishop stood firm on the convent steps, warned the would-be terrorists about the willing Irish defenders, and was able to scare the Know-Nothings off. A month later, on Christmas Eve, 1855, a similar scene played out in Nashville when members of the

Know-Nothings gathered outside the city's cathedral, St. Mary of the Seven Sorrows, intent on disturbing the celebration of midnight mass. Bishop Miles had been tipped off to the potential riot and warned as many parishioners as he could that mass would be canceled. He also asked friends to patrol the streets to safely head off any parishioners who hadn't gotten the word. Miles himself kept watch outside the church. While the Know-Nothings outside the cathedral continued to shout profanities and epithets, they eventually disbanded, realizing their plot had been somewhat foiled. Christmas Eve mass was eventually celebrated. The faithful would not be dissuaded by fear.[21]

East of the state in Knoxville, William Ganaway "Parson" Brownlow led the Know-Nothing movement. A former circuit-riding Methodist minister turned controversial newspaper editor, he published *Brownlow's Knoxville Whig*. After learning that the Catholic Church had purchased land for a church, he published this editorial on March 10, 1855:

> In all communities, Catholics are to be found who are good citizens, but in general, they are a dangerous population much to be dreaded. They will drink, swear, like, fight, break the sabbath, and for a trifling consideration get their sins pardoned by a presumptuous and arrogant Priest! In all communities there are those who will flatter these people, and from selfish motives seek to win their favor. We will not be found among that number—we are too much of a Know Nothing in sentiment.[22]

The Know-Nothing Party's influence mostly waned by the middle and late 1850s as a new upstart party, the Republicans, shifted the focus of the country toward other issues, most significantly slavery and the tension leading up to the Civil War. By 1860, the party had all but vanished. "Division between North and South, which nativists endeavored to submerge, soon submerged nativism," noted John

Higham in *Strangers in the Land*. "The anti-foreign crusade could not prevail against sectional forces which were themselves evolving into overriding loyalties."[23] In other words, you can only have one enemy at a time.

"We thank God that we no longer have to go in disguise when we leave our convent grounds as we did in those days of the reign of the 'Know-Nothings' and 'Nativists' and other bigots," wrote a Dominican Sister called to serve at the new St. Cecilia Academy in Nashville in the late 1850s. "How Blessed we are! Please God may we never have to go under cover again, and may we always be able to stand for what we are!"[24]

Helpful for Roman Catholics in Tennessee in the mid-1850s was having Bishop Miles at their helm, "a man of wisdom, patience, and education," notes historian Garvin Davenport, "who could maintain his dignity in the midst of intolerant attacks and soon won the confidence and the friendship of many broad-minded Protestant leaders."[25] His cool headedness during the potential of a riot during midnight mass was evidence of that. In Tennessee, Orengo took his lead from Miles, so it makes sense to imagine that in addition to his modest lunch of cheese and crackers, Orengo carried some goodwill in his saddle bag. Gazzo mentioned that Orengo "was much beloved by both Catholics and Protestants, even though he never hesitated to express his opinions about the errors of the non-Catholic sects." He could also be crafty.

Gazzo told a story about the time a young married man was having a heated disagreement with his wife and sent for Orengo. The wife was not Catholic and refused to have their first child baptized into the faith. They had an argument, and the wife took the child to her parents' house. She refused to live with her husband until he relented. Orengo, "believing that this was a ruse to gain the mastery over her husband," according to Gazzo, told the young man he could fix the problem. The priest found a board, wrote "For Sale" on it, and fastened it to the house. When the wife heard that their home was up for sale, she immediately returned to her husband. Not long after, Orengo baptized both mother and child.

CHAPTER 4

The Growth of St. Patrick's

On January 22, 1852, the Tennessee General Assembly chartered the Nashville and Northwestern Railroad for the "purpose of establishing communication by railroad between Nashville and the Mississippi River, beginning at Nashville and terminating on the Mississippi River in Obion County."[1] The route for the railroad would come from Nashville directly through Humphreys County, only a couple of miles from where St. Patrick's had been established, and continue on to the Tennessee River at Johnsonville. The railroad would be built simultaneously from the west and the east. The clearing of land for the railroad construction provided an opportunity to relocate St. Patrick's Church closer to the railroad. On April 16, 1856, Orengo bought 640 acres of land from Wm. M. Adcock near the proposed railroad. Under his direction, church parishioners dismantled the existing church structure log by log and moved it to its present-day location near the railroad. The land was flatter, and having been cleared for the new railway, ideal for church construction.[2] The proximity of the community to the railroad eventually brought more settlers to the area. Because of the growing Catholic population and the large number of children in the settlement, Orengo began construction of a school. At its opening later in 1856, St. Patrick's School had two teachers supplied by the Sisters of Mercy in Nashville. More teachers eventually came on and the school thrived. As it was the only school for miles, it served both the Catholic and non-Catholic population. Orengo served as minister, doctor and lawyer to all.[3]

The civil engineer who surveyed the area for the railroad was a man named McEwen who is rumored to have impressed the local group of people living there, so much so that they began to call the place McEwen Station. It was eventually shortened to simply McEwen.

At some point during the move of the church and the erection of the school, what has become known at Saint Patrick's Irish Picnic, home to the World's Largest Pork Barbecue and the oldest continuously running festival in Tennessee, was established.[4] The timeline for the first event is hard to pin down exactly, though Dr. Kristen Bradley—lifelong resident of Humphreys County, descendant of McEwen's first Irish immigrant settlers, alumnus of St. Patrick's School, and a college professor—posits a likely interpretation in her 2014 dissertation on the event.[5] In preparation for the move of the church, Orengo and St. Patrick's parishioners desired a bell for the church in its new location to inform parishioners that mass was beginning. The idea for a fundraiser was hatched. Local farmers brought sheep, goats, and pigs to cook and sell to what were mostly railroad workers and their families in the community. As land was continually being cleared, there was plenty of hickory wood to cook with. It was so successful the first time, current St. Patrick's parishioners told Bradley, that they did it again. By the third year, it became a fundraiser for the school, which it remains to this day.

While erecting a new church and school and planning a major fundraising event kept Orengo busy, he nevertheless maintained an exhaustive missionary schedule during the mid-1850s. He continued to attend to the parishioners in Clarksville at what was now named Immaculate Conception Church, as well as the missions in Dover,

FIGURE 4.1. The author with the Tennessee Historical Commission historical marker recognizing Fr. Orengo and the establishment of St. Patrick's in McEwen, Tennessee. Photo: Barbara Hooper

Lebanon, Charlotte, and Sycamore Mills, near present-day Ashland City in Cheatham County. He also started to minister to Catholics, mostly Irish immigrants, working on the Gallatin and Louisville Railroad line. In 1855, in addition to St. Patrick's in Humphrey's County, he was traveling to Columbia, Franklin, Murfreesboro, Dover, and Perryville, a new mission on the Tennessee River about sixty miles southwest of McEwen. It's a circuit Orengo kept up into 1856.[6]

St. Patrick's Irish Picnic and Barbara Hooper

I visited the Irish Picnic for the first time in 2024, when it was celebrating its 170th anniversary. On a weather-perfect July day, my family and I had what might be the best pulled pork we've ever had. At $15 a plate with sides and a dessert for adults and $8 for children, it was certainly the most affordable. We played every game available, from a ring toss to win a two-liter bottle of soda, to tic-tac-toe that was impossible to lose—at least for my daughters, who attendants really wouldn't let lose—with a softball-size Wiffle Ball. Among the musical performers was Tayla Lynn, granddaughter of country music legend Loretta Lynn. Tayla Lynn's children went to St. Patrick's and she continues to support the school. Inside the parish offices, a display was set up honoring the history of the parish and the picnic. While there were Dominican Sisters milling around the festival, the more than ten thousand people who attend it each year indicate that it's not only a festival for the area's Catholics. It's a town, county, and regional-wide celebration of community. I found Barbara Hooper, volunteer extraordinaire and president of the Society of St. Vincent de Paul's Conference at St. Patrick's, making the rounds in the dining hall and holding court at the barbecue pits. I had visited Hooper earlier in the year to look at the church's archives and talk about St. Patrick's and Orengo. We had lunch that day—catfish, white beans, greens—a few blocks away from the church at a gas station market. Hooper knew everyone, and everyone knew Hooper. She is clearly the glue of the community. "She's our Mary Catherine Strobel," Ted Rice, director of the Humphreys County Museum and Civil War Fort, told me. Mary Catherine Strobel, a Nashville native who grew up in what is now the Germantown neighborhood of the city, is best remembered in Middle Tennessee for her tireless, joyful commitment to the poor, the sick, and the homeless. She was the mother of four children, most notably the beloved Nashville Catholic priest Fr. Charles Strobel, founder of the renowned Room in the Inn shelter program for the unhoused. Following her death in 1986, the United Way in Nashville posthumously honored her with the first Mary Catherine Strobel Volunteer of the Year Award.[7] Given to volunteers from throughout

Middle Tennessee who quietly and selflessly give to others every day of their lives, the award has been given out every year since.

Hooper and the Society of St. Vincent de Paul's Conference at St. Patrick's were finalists for the Mary Catherine Strobel Award in 2005. They were just getting started and didn't win, but they did pick up a big award in September 2022: the Emerging Leaders Award at the Society of St. Vincent de Paul's Annual Conference in Baltimore, Maryland. They were honored for their work providing emergency disaster relief in Humphreys County following the devastating floods that wrecked the area in August 2021, displacing hundreds of families and killing twenty people. Hooper and her St. Vincent de Paul colleague Eddie Bozman helped more than one hundred families get back into their homes by supplying furnishings, supplies for construction work and general support.

Hooper is a descendant of McEwen's first settlers and St. Patrick's first parishioners; Irish immigrants who toiled alongside Orengo to build the area's Catholic community. Her ancestors, Thomas Tarpy and Mary Herity, were the last people Orengo married at St. Patrick's before his missions in the area ended. She grew up in a family with priests and sisters and has been involved in the church in one way or another her entire life. She was baptized at St. Patrick's, received all her sacraments there, and was married there. Her father was the first, she believes, to have a true Irish wake at the church. She's been working with the Society of St. Vincent de Paul for almost twenty years, volunteering originally because she wanted to encourage children to read at mass. I tell Hooper that while it's nice to find structures still standing built by Orengo, or to visit churches where he celebrated mass and baptized and married the faithful, she and her tireless ministry for those in need is a living connection to the priest and his true legacy.

"I don't know why I do what I do," she tells me. "I guess I do what I do because maybe that's what God wants me to do. Or my ancestors

FIGURE 4.2. Barbara Hooper with the author in 2024 at St. Patrick's Catholic Church in McEwen, Tennessee. Hooper is a descendant of the area's original settlers and founders of the church. She currently serves the community as president of the parish's conference of the Saint Vincent de Paul Society. Photo courtesy of the author.

are pushing me, saying 'hey, this is what you have to do.' I guess you can call it gut feeling, but then you realize that's not what it is. It's God's providence."

When I reconnected with Hooper a few months after the picnic, she told me about a retreat she just completed to teach teenagers in the community about homelessness. Similar to programs often held for adults, where they might spend the night out on the street or on the steps of city hall, the teenagers lived in cardboard homes of their own construction. They had a simple vessel and utensil with which to eat and learned about homelessness from advocates for the unhoused. She called it the Ozanam retreat after Society of St. Vincent de Paul founder Frederic Ozanam. Following the retreat, on the grounds of St. Patrick's where the Irish Picnic is held, she hosted a Halloween "Trunk and Treat" and "Touch-a-Truck" event for as many as 1,500 children in partnership with the local Baptist and Methodist Churches. She was already preparing for the parish's "Neighbor in Need" Christmas program, where food and gifts will be gathered for hundreds in the community. All the while, she counsels whoever is in need, whether it's those in the car line to pick up food from the Society's food pantry, a man whose wife attempted suicide, or someone grieving over the death of their mother.

"Sometimes just to go and give somebody a hug and let them know that somebody cares about them is all you can do," she says.

The story that Hooper tells me that sticks with me the most is about the day at mass that she realized that the priest didn't have any altar servers. "The priest had no one," she says. "I was there with my family, and I don't know what made me get up and do it, but it just hit me, 'Jesus is alone, and so is the priest.' I got up, bowed, and went up and served."

CHAPTER 5

A Death in Memphis

On September 17, 1855, exposure to yellow fever in Memphis took the life of St. Peter's parish priest Fr. John R. Cleary, OP, making him the first priest in Tennessee to die of the disease and one of 220 persons who lost their lives in the second iteration of the epidemic in the city.[1] It would act as prelude to the havoc that the disease would wreak on Memphis, its Catholics, and clergy some twenty years later in the 1870s.[2] Cleary was a curate serving under the direction of Orengo's friend, Fr. Thomas Grace, the pastor of St. Peter's. Cleary possessed a similar zeal to Orengo. "Father Cleary did not confine his labors to the diocese," wrote Fr. Victor O'Daniel in *The Father of the Church in Tennessee*. "Up and down the majestic Father of the Waters he travelled, laboring among the workmen on the boats, and levees, no less than traversed northwestern Mississippi, eastern Arkansas, and western Tennessee in every direction. . . . He was the soul of charity. The poor were the special object of his tireless ministrations."[3]

Whether he was assigned to Memphis, or volunteered to help, Orengo was quick to risk his health and life and travel to St. Peter's to assist his friend Grace until a successor to Cleary could be found. Entries in the sacramental records book at St. Peter's signed by Orengo date from September 29, 1855, just twelve days after Cleary's death,

FIGURE 5.1. St. Peter's Catholic Church in Memphis in 2024. Photo courtesy of the author.

FIGURE 5.2. View from the choir lot of the nave and sanctuary of St. Peter in Memphis. Photo courtesy of the author.

FIGURE 5.3. The Sacristy in St. Peter's in Memphis in 2024. Photo courtesy of the author.

FIGURE 5.4. A bronze plaque in the Memorial Chapel at St. Peter's in Memphis honors Fr. John R. Cleary, O.P., who died of yellow fever in 1855 and is buried under the sanctuary of the church. Fr. Orengo went to Memphis after Cleary's death to support his friend and pastor Fr. Thomas Grace. Also honored on the plaque and buried under the sanctuary are Fr. James Hyacinth Clarkson, O.P., who died of cholera in 1848, and Fr. Joseph Augustine Kelly, a hero of the yellow fever epidemic in 1878. Photo courtesy of the author.

until November 8, 1855. Orengo was already well known in Memphis and had been to St. Peter's many times to celebrate mass and baptisms in the original brick structure completed in 1843. A July 10, 1887, article on the history of Churches in Memphis even lists Orengo as among the priests "in charge" of the parish.[4] Imagine the range of emotions Orengo must have felt on returning to the city under such dire circumstances to celebrate mass in St. Peter's new building, an extraordinary fortress-like structure of Norman Gothic style by noted Roman Catholic Church architect Patrick Charles Keely, a designer of more than six hundred churches in the United States, including every nineteenth-century Catholic cathedral in New England.[5] As the work on the church had begun in 1852, Orengo had surely seen and been aware of its progress. Its completion had to be unlike any place he had been in Tennessee, save for St. Mary of the Seven Sorrows in Nashville. St. Peter's dwarfed even that. The roomy and warm wood-paneled sacristy must have provided a welcome respite from his journey on horseback from the multitude of places he might have been before being called to Memphis to assist Grace.

St. Peter's, on the corner of present-day B. B. King Boulevard and Adams Avenue in downtown Memphis, still thrives today and continues to be served by the Dominican Order. It is listed on the National Register of Historic Places. Fr. Cleary is buried under the sanctuary of the church, along with Fr. James Hyacinth Clarkson, OP, who died of cholera in 1848, and Fr. Joseph Augustine Kelly, a hero of the yellow fever epidemic in 1878. A bronze plaque honoring all three priests is located in the Memorial Chapel in the west transept.[6]

Orengo maintained a busy schedule through the remainder of the 1850s, continuing to minister to the faithful at St. Patrick's in McEwen, Immaculate Conception in Clarksville, and the missions in Columbia, Franklin, Murfreesboro, and Perryville. It's possible he even made a trip back to Memphis to wish his dear friend Grace well on his appointment as the Bishop of the Diocese of St. Paul,

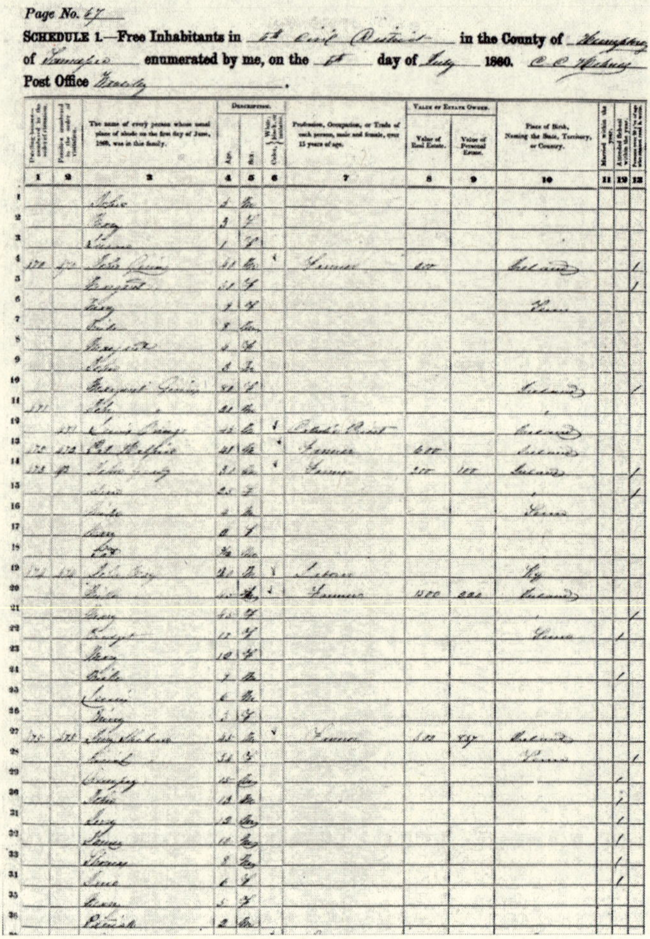
Page No. 67
SCHEDULE 1.—Free Inhabitants in 5th Civil District in the County of Humphreys of Tennessee enumerated by me, on the 5th day of July 1860.
Post Office

FIGURE 5.5. The 1860 census has Fr. "Lewis" Orengo living in Humphreys County, Tennessee, and his country of origin as "Ireland."

Minnesota, before Grace said his final mass at St. Peter's on July 12, 1859. *The Memphis Daily Appeal* acknowledged Grace's impact on the city before his departure, noting that "His ministry has not only been an able one, but has been attended with almost unexampled success."[7]

By 1860, Orengo had to feel he was making an impact. His former parish in Clarksville, Immaculate Conception, where he had served as resident priest from 1848 to 1855, opened its first school. To Orengo's delight, the parishioners honored their former priest by naming the school for him: St. Aloysius School for Boys and Girls.[8] It remained St. Aloysious until 1880, when after moving to a new location, it was renamed St. Mary's School in reference to the history of the parish's first name.[9] Orengo also began to settle in and call St. Patrick's and McEwen home. The July 6, 1860, census has him listed as living in District 6, Humphreys, Tennessee, USA, in dwelling number 471, and his occupation as "Catholic Priest." Curiously, his country of origin is listed as Ireland, perhaps noted in error by the census taker, who assumed everyone was from Ireland or thought "Orengo" sounded Irish. Or maybe that was Orengo's way of being in solidarity with his parishioners. Listed as living with him in this district are twenty-three white males and seventeen white females, eleven of whom are foreign born.[10]

The comfort of calling McEwen home, however, would not last long. Changes would come in the next decade that would have profound effects on Orengo's ministry, on the parishioners of St. Patrick's, on Tennessee, and ultimately, the entire country.

CHAPTER 6

A Farewell to Bishop Miles

By the late 1850s, Nashville Bishop Richard Pius Miles's health was in decline. The man who brought Orengo to Tennessee and was responsible for so much of Catholicism's growth in the state since its designation as a diocese in 1837 could no longer serve the Catholics of Tennessee on his own. He'd been petitioning Rome for some time to appoint a coadjutor of the diocese. His hope was to find someone to both share his duties and prepare to be his successor. He got that wish on March 15, 1859, when a fellow Dominican, Fr. James Whelan, OP, was appointed coadjutor. Whelan was installed a few weeks later, May 29, 1859, in a mass at the cathedral, St. Mary of the Seven Sorrows, presided over by Bishop Miles. "I cheerfully surrender to him," Miles was recorded as saying, "as well the consolations as the labors, cares, and responsibilities of the Episcopapacy. I give up to him all but my title and chair, which I am not at liberty to relinquish while I live." While there is no record of Orengo specifically attending the installation mass, it's possible he was among the "several attendant priests and acolytes" reported by Fr. Henry Vincent Brown of Chattanooga in his account for the *Louisville Guardian* a week later.[1] Plus, Whelan and Orengo knew each other. Whelan was a novitiate of St.

Joseph's Province in Ohio when Orengo arrived in the United States in 1845, and took his final orders there in 1846, when Orengo was serving in their sister province at St. Rose in Kentucky.

While he was able to preside over the dedication of the corner stone of the new Church of the Assumption of the Blessed Virgin Mary in what is now the Germantown area of Nashville on August 14, 1859, Miles's health worsened over the next nine months, and on the afternoon of February 21, 1860, after being given last rites by Whelan, Miles died quietly at home in Nashville. The cause was listed as apoplexy.[2] The Bishop's body was laid out in state at St. Mary's the following day, Ash Wednesday, as a crowd of people arrived to pay their respects.[3] The funeral mass was held that Friday, February 24, celebrated by Whelan with the Very Reverend B. J. Spalding of Louisville as assistant priest. Various news accounts mentioned several priests in attendance, including Fr. Brown and Fr. D'Arco, the latter having traveled with Orengo from Italy in 1845. But no mention of Orengo. I like to think he was there, though, to see his dear friend off. I can't imagine it any other way.

Miles's accomplishments as bishop cannot be overstated. He started with very little, and because of the relatively few Catholics in Tennessee, forged forward with very little support by the Catholic leadership in the country. There was Protestant bigotry and hostility to contend with, and creditors who were never satisfied.[4] But what he did was remarkable. By the time of his death, the Diocese of Nashville included thirteen full-time priests, fourteen churches completed or under construction, thirty missionary stations, three communities of women religious, one academy for girls close to completion (St. Cecilia), nine schools, and one orphanage. It is estimated that there were some twelve thousand Catholics in Tennessee.

After his death, Bishop Miles's remains were buried beneath the high altar at St. Mary's. In 1972, the cast iron casket containing his remains was moved to a small chapel in the church's northwest corner, where it remains today. At the time of the relocation, Miles's remains were deemed to be "incorrupt," a Catholic distinction that means a body, or a part of a body, has experienced little to no decomposition after death. It's considered a sign of holiness or preparation for resurrection.

CHAPTER 7

The Railroad and the War

Through the second half of the 1850s, work continued on the railroad lines that would connect Middle and West Tennessee, albeit slowly. While some progress was being made on the west side of the Tennessee River, problems in 1858 with funding for the Nashville and Northwestern Railroad meant a slowdown for the crucial connection on the east side between the city and the river and especially for the drawbridge over the waterway. When Tennessee voted to leave the Union in June 1861, only six miles of the railroad had been completed from the river eastward, and only twenty-eight miles from Nashville to Kingston Springs westward, meaning there was still quite a bit to go before the railroad would meet in McEwen.

After Fort Henry and Fort Donelson fell to the Union in early February of 1862, the Union now had dominion over traffic on the Cumberland and Tennessee Rivers. That meant control of Middle and West Tennessee. They occupied the state capitol by the end of the month.

The completion of the stalled Nashville and Northwestern Railroad was now a renewed priority, needed by the Union to transfer supplies to and from Nashville and Johnsonville on the Tennessee River. Work resumed by the federal government on September 7, 1863,

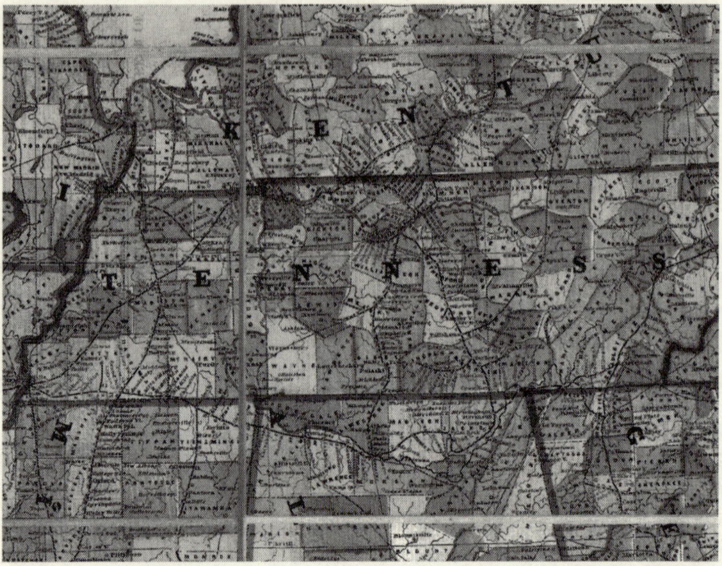

FIGURE 7.1. Detail of map of Tennessee railroads, their stations and distances, published by James T. Lloyd and Millard Fillmore, New York, 1862. Library of Congress, Geography and Map Division.

with the same plan the railroad originally had, to come from both the east and west and meet in the middle, around McEwen.[1] Many of the Union troops who worked on the railroad, which included members of the United State Colored Troops (USCT), camped at fortifications around McEwen and Waverly, in Humphreys County.[2] Construction of the railroad needed to be guarded by Union soldiers around the clock to protect against any Confederate attack. Additionally, once the Johnsonville Depot on the Tennessee River was ready, the railroad remained under persistent attack by rebels.[3]

While Orengo might have been able to travel by rail to some extent in the new decade, he was either still on horseback or walking once he reached the end of a line. When the Civil War broke out in 1861, travel in the area got dangerous.

In 1910, C. W. Russell, then living at the Old Mason's Home in Shelbyville, Kentucky, wrote a letter to Fr. John K. Larkin in Johnson City, Tennessee. He had read in the *Catholic Record* of Louisville that Larkin was writing a history of the Catholic Church in Tennessee. He had a story he wanted to share.

> Before the Civil War I was an engineer running construction trains, building track from Clarksville to Paris. A young Priest used to ride with me in the cab, once a month, to the end of the track. I knew when he left me each time he was going into dangerous territory. I offered him my Derringer.[4] He declined, but said he would ask the Bishop as he could see the danger involved. The Bishop did not think it best. I insisted that he take care of the pistol for me. He would not.
>
> I heard afterwards that he had been murdered; and the war came on, and I heard no more of him. . . . The Priest was a most pleasant young gentleman named Orengo, and I loved him.[5]

There's a lot to consider in this letter. First, while there are plenty of historical references and oral histories of people's affections for Orengo, there are none as explicit as this. Russell was in his seventies when he wrote the letter, living in the Old Mason's Home in Shelbyville, remembering someone he had met while working on the railroad almost fifty years earlier. It's clear Orengo had made an impression. The note about Orengo refusing Russell's pistol for protection, deflecting instead to the purview of his bishop, speaks to Orengo's peaceful nature and reliance on his wits. And while the story doesn't particularly speak to Orengo in McEwen—there were missions in Paris and elsewhere he could have been attending, or getting off at Erin and making his way south to McEwen—it offers a piece to the puzzle of Orengo's experience as the war ramped up, leading to why Orengo would eventually leave McEwen for a time and stay in Nashville, a considerably more protected city, instead of roaming around in far west Middle or West Tennessee.

Parish histories of this period say that in McEwen, Orengo's life was threatened by guerrillas and bushwhackers. Evidence of the lawlessness in the area at the time can be found in the files of the Southern Claims Commission, which allowed Southern Unionist citizens to seek compensation for property that had been taken or damaged by the US Army during the Civil War. Thomas Langan, a postmaster and resident of McEwen during the war, filed a Southern Commission Claim in 1876.[6] While the federal government chose only to reimburse Langan $138.56 of the $682.06 that he claimed, the summary on the claim by the commissioner who handled it says that the naturalized Irish immigrant "was much threatened and molested by rebel bushwackers . . . because he was known as a Union man. His house was robbed. He was taken out and threatened with hanging. The rebels set fire to his house twice." Langan's sworn testimony goes into vivid detail about being dragged out of his house, forced to go to his stables to free a mule, his family being threatened and molested, and a gun being pointed at his head. "I was several times told that they intended to kill that old Union Irishman," the commissioner writes.

Among others listed on the claim who offered testimony were St. Patrick's parishioners James Sheehy and Thomas Tarpy, an ancestor of Barbara Hooper.

What the commission ultimately allowed was reimbursement for wood boards, Irish potatoes, pork, and twelve "fat" hogs that it appears Union General Henry Thomas and his troops took as they passed through the area. While the Battle of Nashville raged, and no Federal troops were in the area, things apparently got worse for Langan. In his testimony, as part of the eighty-point questionnaire claimants needed to fill out to prove they were Union loyalists, Langan notes of the bushwackers:

> They took a good mule, they took 60 dollars . . . they rifled (through) my house generally and took a good many things . . . the things were taken during the Battle of Nashville when there were no Federal Troops here. . . . I never received any pay for any of it, they also took 40 dollars worth of postage stamps from me that belonged to the U.S. Government. . . . They also took a Revolver, a Doubled Barreled shot(gun), a Dueling pistol, and bed clothes and saddles, besides some other trinkets.

It wasn't only "rebel bushwackers" making things difficult for Orengo and the parishioners of St. Patrick's.

Fr. Gazzo, in the oral history recorded by O'Daniel, told this Civil War–era story about an Orengo run-in with Union soldiers.

> [Fr. Orengo] was halted by soldiers who demanded his horse. The quick-witted Italian priest replied: "I am on a sick-call; and the person I am going to see is very ill. To know you would not wish to delay such an errand of mercy and charity." "Wait here," said one of the men, "until I see the officer about this matter." But when he started for the officer, Father Orengo, knowing that his steed was fleet, dashed off in the other direction. He knew that the soldiers would soon pursue him. So when he reached a turn in the road that shut him off from their sight, he wheeled into a field of tall corn, and alighted at a distance from the thoroughfare. While on the ground he patted his horse to keep him from neighing. Soon he heard the patter of hoofs in hot chase after him. When they had passed, he mounted his horse again, and made for the woods and thickets. Although his clothes were torn almost to threads, he saved his faithful horse, and perhaps his life.

By 1863, it simply wasn't safe or feasible for Orengo to be in McEwen or on his missionary rounds. He instead went to Nashville.

A June 6, 1863, article in *The Freeman's Journal* by "Charlie," its Nashville correspondent for the war, reports on Orengo coming to Nashville.

> Rev. Fr. Orengo came up from Dixie on Saturday. His parish is stationed about 20 miles south of this, at a place called the Irish Settlement, and in 'business times' he had a large and important field of labor. He has now, however, but a few old men and women and children. The country is thoroughly devastated, and the finishing stroke was given by the Federals, on a recent visit, destroying all the implements of farming, manufacturing, etc., leaving the poor people in a very destitute condition.[7]

The Freeman's Journal was a New York weekly sympathetic to the Confederate cause, and "Charlie" was Edward E. Jones, a prominent newspaperman in Nashville.[8] While the reporting certainly could be slanted, Southern Commission claims do confirm damage in the area by both the Union Army and Confederate rebels. And while Southern Commission claimant Thomas Langan was a Union loyalist, there were also people at McEwen and St. Patrick's who were surely Confederate supporters, especially those families of enlisted men who had either volunteered to join the Confederate army or were drafted as part of the Confederate Conscription Act of 1862.[9] Young men had left the area to join other Irish immigrants and descendants from Giles, Davidson, and Montgomery Counties to organize as the 10th Tennessee Infantry Regiment of the Confederate army at Fort Henry in 1861. They were soon nicknamed "The Bloody Tenth" after suffering heavy losses at the Battle of Fort Donelson in 1862. Able-bodied older men, some of whom had children fighting in the war, worked alongside soldiers and impressed Black laborers building the Johnsonville Supply Depot west of McEwen on the Tennessee River.[10] St. Patrick's had been significantly depleted of its parishioners.

FIGURE 8.1. St. Mary of the Seven Sorrows in Nashville, Tennessee, as it stands today. Photo courtesy of the author.
FIGURE 8.2. View of the nave and sanctuary at St. Mary of the Seven Sorrows in Nashville. Photo courtesy of the author.

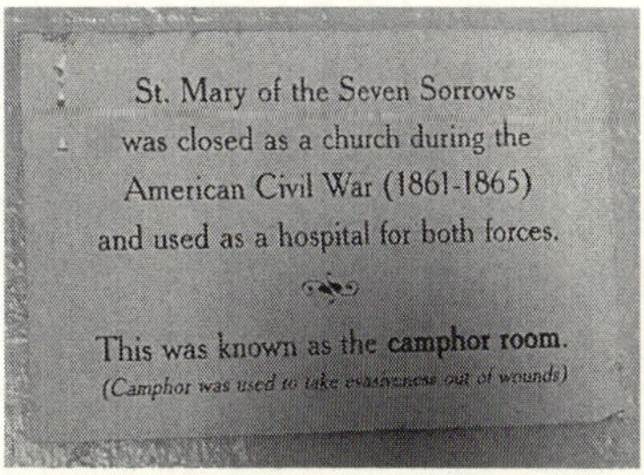

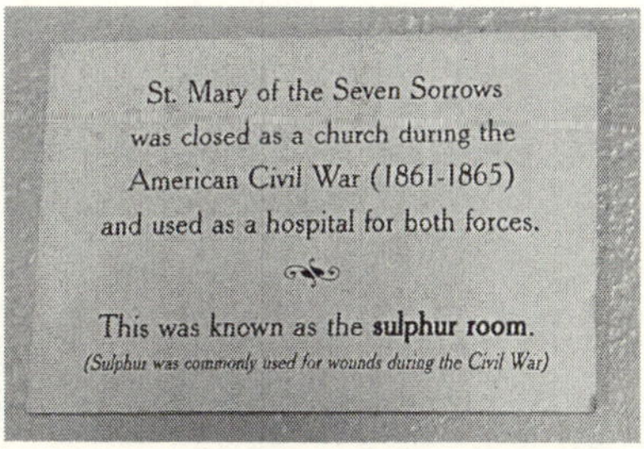

FIGURES 8.3 AND 8.4. Signs marking the camphor and sulphur rooms used during the Civil War at St. Mary of the Seven Sorrows in Nashville. Photo courtesy of the author.

This was not unique. In general, 1863 was a difficult year for everyone in the state. Bereft of young men who left to join the Confederate army, only about half of the churches in the state continued to hold services. Within a year, most congregations were disrupted in some capacity.[11]

Did Orengo have a position or loyalty to either side in the Civil War? It doesn't seem so. He appears to have ministered where he was needed. "Priests ministered on both sides of the divide, and sometimes ministered to soldiers of both armies," notes Fr. John Vidmar, OP, in his history of St. Joseph Province, noting that the province was in a tenuous geographical position, with priests and priories in Ohio, Kentucky, and Tennessee. Those who ministered to troops as they passed through their parish areas included Orengo.[12] In Nashville, where Orengo spent a good portion of 1863 and '64, it was mostly Union troops, especially during the period of the Battle of Nashville when St. Mary's was converted briefly into a hospital in 1864.[13]

That was not the stance of Fr. Emmeran Bliemel, OSB, the pastor of the Church of the Assumption of the Blessed Virgin Mary in Nashville, and the priest Bishop Whelan assigned to St. Patrick's after Orengo left. Bliemel was a Confederate sympathizer, which was common knowledge to those around him. He at one point was even arrested by Union General William Starke Rosecrans on suspicion of being "Charlie," the pro-Confederate Nashville correspondent for *The Freeman's Journal*. Bliemel wanted desperately to be with the 10th Tennessee Infantry Regiment and had been petitioning Bishop Whelan to send him somewhere where he could be close to them. When the 10th was reorganized in the fall of 1862 in Mississippi, Bliemel was even nominally appointed its chaplain, even though he was still in Nashville. A year later, in the fall of 1863, when the 10th took a terrible defeat at Chickamauga and Orengo left McEwen, Bliemel had his chance. He made a plea to Whelan to go to McEwen and his request was granted.

FIGURE 8.5. The sulphur room today. Photo courtesy of the author.

Getting there wasn't easy. The 10th Tennessee at the time was encamped in the vicinity of Chattanooga. Travel south on main roads was forbidden and passenger service on available railroads was suspended. He'd have to take a horse. His credentials from the Diocese of Nashville, stating that he was a priest in good standing on his way to McEwen to replace Orengo for a time, were his ticket for safe passage.

> Nashville Cathedral, Oct. 6, 1863—The bearer, the Rev. Emmeran Bliemel is a zealous, worthy priest of the diocese in good standing and with full faculties he goes for a time to Humphreys county to take the place of Father Orengo. It may be necessary for him to pass beyond that point or even go out of Tennessee, in which case I can recommend him to such ecclesiastical authorities as he may meet with as a Missionary worthy of their support and confidence—H.V. Brown, V.G. and Rector.

The only risk was that an astute Union soldier might notice that the Vicar General of the Nashville Diocese who signed the credential, Fr. Henry Brown, was the former chaplain of the 10th Tennessee before its loss at Fort Donelson; the same Fr. Brown who acted as correspondent for Whelan's installation mass as co-adjutor of the diocese in 1859, and was later reported to have attended Bishop Miles's funeral. Did Orengo and Bliemel know each other, or at least cross paths? Bliemel's last baptism at St. Mary's was October 4, 1863. Orengo's first recorded baptism was a week later, on October 11. Did Orengo give Bliemel any insight into the parishioners of St. Patrick's or what the war climate was in McEwen? Did Bliemel even want it? It's unlikely, for both Bliemel and Brown knew the passage to McEwen was only an excuse to get Bliemel out of Nashville and to his regiment.

Once Bliemel got to McEwen, where the families of some members of the 10th still resided, he didn't stay long. He got a new horse, headed west, then south and east to make his way across the state line into Georgia. On November 1, 1863, he presented his letter to Augustin Verot, the Bishop of the Diocese of Savannah, and was granted permission to serve as a missionary in the area. By January, he was formally nominated Chaplain by Confederate Colonel William Grace and on March 3, 1864, was officially named Chaplain of the 10th Tennessee. He served with the regiment throughout the year until his death at the Battle of Jonesboro on August 31. While ministering the last rites to Colonel Grace, who had gone down during heavy Union fire, he was decapitated by what was likely a cannonball. He was only the second American Catholic priest to be killed in combat—Fr. Anthony Rey, SJ, being the first in the Mexican-American War—and the only Catholic priest to be killed in battle in the Civil War.[14]

Originally buried at the Patrick Cleburne Confederate Cemetery in Jonesboro, Bliemel's remains were eventually transferred to a Benedictine parish in Tuscumbia, Alabama, in 1899.[15] Bliemel was posthumously given the Confederate Medal of Honor in 1984. He is honored with a memorial on the grounds of the historic courthouse in Jonesboro, Georgia, and with a park named in his honor at his Nashville parish, Assumption Church.[16]

CHAPTER 8

Sequestered in Nashville

While in Nashville, Orengo was among several priests assisting at both St. Mary's and the new church of St. John the Evangelist. St. John's was located on the east side of the Cumberland River in what was then a separate incorporated city named Edgefield Junction and is now known as the Edgefield neighborhood of East Nashville.[1] The parish was dedicated on December 22, 1857, with Fr. Ivo Schacht, who preceded Orengo in Clarksville and McEwen, named as pastor. Sacramental records indicate that Orengo recorded a baptism at the church on February 10, 1864.

Orengo would have gone back and forth from St. Mary's in Nashville, on the west side of the Cumberland River, to St. John the Evangelist on the east side in Edgefield Junction via a bridge over the Cumberland River that was built less than a decade earlier. It wasn't the first bridge to span the river. The current structure had replaced the original, built between 1819 and 1823 by Irish immigrants who were among the first significant Catholics to arrive in the area. The Nashville Bridge Company, organized in 1819, contracted with Pittsburgh company Stacker and Johnson to build the bridge, and the company brought with them thirty skilled Irish workers who settled with their families in the area. The workers, all devout Catholics, threatened to leave when they discovered there was no

Catholic Church in the area. The Nashville Bridge Company, apt to appease the workers, appealed to Bishop Joseph Flaget, prelate of the Diocese of Bardstown from 1808 to 1839, to send a priest to serve the workers. Flaget agreed to send Fr. Robert Abell, then assigned to missionary work in Tennessee. The workers quickly erected a small frame church in their off time on what was then known as Cedar Knob.[2] Abell continued to travel from Kentucky and visit the workers every few months, even coming with Bishop Flaget in May 1821 when they stayed with the famous French Canadian and Nashville's "first citizen," Timothy Demonbreun, in his house on what is now 3rd Street in downtown Nashville. It is believed it was at that time that the first mass celebrated by a bishop in Tennessee was celebrated by Flaget in Demonbreun's home.

Abel was assigned to Louisville in 1824, and with the bridge completed by then, the Irish bridge builders moved on to other work. The frame church structure on Cedar Knob began to fall into disrepair for lack of use, though for a brief time it was used as a prep school. Its fortunes changed in the late 1820s when efforts were made to assign priests to the city more often to serve its Catholics. Fr. James Cosgrave (also written in some accounts as Cosgreve) from the Diocese of Charleston, South Carolina, was assigned as pastor and work slowly began to replace the frame structure with a sturdier brick one. Cosgrave was a man of ingenuity. There are news reports of masses being held in the building, "the Church being yet in a very unfinished state," with collections held "for further means to finish the interior of the building."[3] Lottery tickets were sold in a fundraising effort. The Easter Sunday service in May 1828 was a grand affair complete with a concert. General Andrew Jackson was in attendance.[4] The brick structure was completed by 1830 and named Holy Rosary Cathedral. It was in this church in 1838 that Bishop Miles was formally installed as the first Bishop of the Diocese of Nashville. In 1843, Holy Rosary was dismantled after its land was sold to the State of Tennessee and selected as the location of the Tennessee state capitol. Construction of a new cathedral, St. Mary of the Seven Sorrows, began shortly after in 1844 and was completed in 1848. The legacy of those Irish Catholic bridgebuilders, and the zeal of Fr. Cosgrave, however, is not entirely lost to history. The bricks from the dismantled church were salvaged and used to build Assumption Church in Germantown in 1859. The buttress of the original bridge can still be seen on the west side of the Cumberland River underneath what is now the Woodland Street Bridge. An interpretative panel tells its story, including the fact that in the late 1830s, thousands of Cherokees crossed the bridge on the Trail of Tears.[5] A historic marker was installed by the Tennessee Historical Commission on Capitol Hill in 1974, very near James K. Polk and Sarah Polk's grave, acknowledging the site of Holy Rosary Cathedral and the labor of the Irish Catholic workers.[6]

By 1864, after four tumultuous years leading the Diocese of Nashville through the Civil War and massive debt, Bishop Whelan was nearing a breaking point. His troubles were piling up in accusations of insobriety and fear and anxiety over his political position. The city may have been occupied, but Confederate supporters in the city were none too pleased with what they perceived as Whelan's friendship with Union General, and devout Catholic, William Starke Rosecrans. Nor did they like his apparent acquiescence to Federal troops. A sermon Whelan had preached before Union troops arrived in the city, in which he told his congregation that regardless of what happens they must put their trust in God and not forget their religion, was perceived by some as pro-Union. While it might appear that Whelan was run out of town when he resigned as both bishop of Nashville and the pastor of the St. Mary's, a report on the diocese prepared by Whelan in June of 1863 gives a more clear-eyed indication of both the financial hand he was dealt when becoming the bishop, and the challenges the war presented. He sounds exhausted. He complains of the debt incurred by the building of the Church of the Assumption, a church he says, "was built in an out of the way place, and accessible to 6 or 8 families of Germans."[7] He adds that there is no congregation to attend this church and that "it never did, and I presume, will not support a pastor even at a salary of two hundred dollars per annum." Whelan writes of doing the best he could under those circumstances and even keeping a priest in his own house (presumably Bliemel) and furnishing him with boarding. And then there was the new parish across the river in Edgefield Junction, the land for which Whelan says was purchased by Fr. Ivo Schacht, who deeded "one miserable corner to Bishop Miles" even though he "never had a deed or title of any kind." All of this meant that after the church was built, Bishop Miles was essentially being extorted by the land's actual owners. Whelan inherited the mess and was eventually able to secure the church after a public auction. He seems disgusted over the whole ordeal in the report, noting that now "the church is attended occasionally from Nashville," Orengo being one of the priests, but since the start of the Civil War, "there is not much of a congregation."

Much of the report is an accounting of the diocese's dire financial situation—the "deplorable" condition of the bishop's residence and the incompleteness of the cathedral among the outstanding expenses—with numerous mentions of the impact of the war. Writes Whelan: "It is to be understood that the Catholics of Nashville are poor, and not very generous at the best of the times, but the breakout of political troubles, rendered impossible to do more in the way of collecting either at home or in any other place."

All of this may be true, though none of it was through the fault of Miles. He did the best with what he had. Miles himself admitted that the bishop's residence was a "rat-trap." It was all he could afford after selling the previous and more spacious residence on Summer St., next to St. Mary's, in 1855 to pay down the diocese debt and support his school and hospital ministries.

Perhaps the only bright spot in the report is Whelan's pride at the cofounding and funding with Miles of St. Cecilia's Academy for Girls in 1860 by the Dominican Sisters of St. Mary from Somerset, Ohio.

> Knowing that a first-class Academy, such as only Catholic Sisters can conduct, would do an immensity of good, and be liberally supported, I spared no labor, no pains, no necessary expenses to ensure the accomplishment of the undertaking. It soon became evident, that my efforts would be crowned with success, and I am happy to be able to say, that St. Cecilia's Academy, near Nashville, is now a permanent institution of the South West, and has already secured the patronage of an extensive and wealthy portion of the country, where a Catholic system of education is not much appreciated.

Even the war—after Nashville fell in 1862 and Confederates evacuated the city, Union troops set up camp on the campus of St. Celicia—cannot tamp down his enthusiasm.

> It must be understood, that the breaking out of the war in 1861 after the commencement of the new building, the blockade, the precarious state of currency, the great price of things, etc. and the disturbed sense of society in general until this time, rendered the undertaking one of no small anxiety. We had commenced, however, and were bound to persevere. Our school was never interrupted for more than about two weeks at the time of the great Stampede of February, 1862.

After Whelan's departure, Fr. Henry V. Brown, who knew Whelan a decade earlier when both used to travel together to Knoxville, was appointed temporary pastor of the cathedral until a new bishop could be installed. Brown was appointed Knoxville's first resident priest in

1852 and before long was serving both Knoxville and Chattanooga and erecting the church of Sts. Peter and Paul Parish in the latter. Whelan's departure called him back to Nashville, but also brought him together with Orengo, who was tapped to serve as Brown's associate pastor at the cathedral.[8] They appear to have become close, and perhaps even a support for one another. There is no mention of Orengo and Brown knowing each other previously, when Brown was the Chaplain of the 10th Tennessee at Fort Henry, or in Brown's correspondence about Whelan's installation mass five years earlier, but Orengo is mentioned in a *Nashville Union and American* obituary for Fr. Brown four years later in 1870. "With the beginning of the construction of the Nashville and Chattanooga Railroad, [Fr. Brown] began a migratory missionary life," the article states, "attending the religious wants of the laborers from one end of the line to the other, in conjunction with the indefatigable Father Louis Orengo."[9] Did Orengo's love of the missionary life inspire a return to a similar life for Fr. Brown after the war? Being sequestered in Nashville through most of 1863 and '64 certainly seemed to ignite in Orengo a desire to travel again. By 1865, he made his first visit to the Vaughn's Gap area of southwest Nashville for mass in the home of an Anthony Burns.[10]

CHAPTER 9

A Post-War Return to Missionary Life

On March 9, 1865, a month before the Civil War officially ended, Orengo went to Europe for a time and was replaced by Fr. Fortune as associate pastor at the cathedral. *The Freeman's Journal* reports that "we have lost a very good father, and gained a fortune."[1] Orengo returned to New York on February 7, 1866, on the ship *Cella* from London and made his way back to Nashville. An interesting anecdote about this time: Some fifty years later, Bishop John Baptist Morris of the Diocese of Little Rock, Arkansas, a native of Hendersonville, Tennessee, was asked to be present in Washington, DC, to celebrate the seven hundredth anniversary of the founding of the Dominicans. He sent his regrets but noted that he had "a warm place for the Dominican Order, because one of them baptized me, and another married my father and mother."[2] In 1933, Fr. V. F. O'Daniel, who wrote the histories of St. Joseph Province and Bishop Miles, found the letter in the Dominican archives and wrote to Bishop Morris to ask him whom it might have been that married his parents and baptized him. Bishop Morris responded to Fr. O'Daniel on September 6, 1933. "I was baptized by Father Luigi Orengo," he wrote, "who was a missionary in Tennessee for many years, going as I have often heard

FIGURE 9.1. A photo of Fr. Orengo taken in the studios of Antoine René Trinquart in Paris, likely his trip back to Europe in 1865/1866. Trinquart was a French photographer active in Paris, France, from 1858 to the 1860s.

from Memphis as far as Knoxville and back annually on horseback."[3]

"It is likewise true that my parents were married by a Dominican Father," Bishop Morris continued, "Father M. B. Fortune, who was at that time pastor or assistant at the old Cathedral in Nashville." It was while Orengo was in Europe that Fortune married Morris's parents. Four months after his return to Nashville, on June 30, 1866—according to the records at St. Mary's of the Seven Sorrows—Orengo baptized their first-born, John Baptist Morris.

Four years after that correspondence, Bishop Morris spoke again of the influence of Dominicans like Orengo, not only on his own life, but on Catholicism in Tennessee. Homilizing at the centennial of the Nashville diocese in 1937, in the new Cathedral of the Incarnation erected in 1909, Morris said, "One cannot speak of the Diocese of Nashville without speaking of the Dominicans, because they were for a long time almost the only missionaries in the state, and the diocese is more indebted to the fathers of St. Dominic for its Catholic life than to any other source whatsoever."[4]

There's also a bit of mystery during this period. There is a record from 1866 of Orengo visiting Emigrant Saving Bank in New York City. Emigrant, which still exists today, was established in 1850 on Chambers Street in New York City. It was created by the Irish Emigrant Society, which was founded in 1841 for the protection of immigrants from Ireland. The bank offered a place for Irish immigrants, and eventually other immigrants, to keep their money safe and send money home to relatives in the old country. Orengo appears to have used their services. In the records for May 19, 1866, under the signature line in the ledger, it says, "Louis, Orengo, The Order of the Dominicans" with residence listed as "Cathedral, Nashville, Tenn."

Under the notes there is this: "In case of sudden death, he wishes any money in the bank be sent to his mother, Bianca Orengo, Castel Vittorio, Italy, Diocese of Ventimiglia. He is about to sail for Italy tomorrow. His instructions are in case of his death the interest on his money is to be paid to his mother and the principal is to go to the superior general of the Order of St. Dominic."[5]

The next day was May 20, 1866. There is no passenger list record of Orengo returning on a ship that would have allowed him to get back to Nashville by June 3, 1866, when sacramental records from St. Mary's indicate he celebrated a baptism. Did he never get on the boat? The other possibility is that he wasn't in New York at all. While most of the records in the ledger appear written by the same hand, likely a clerk at the bank, Orengo's name is written by his own hand,

and appears to be cut from another document, perhaps a letter, and pasted into the book. Names and other pertinent information about the individuals conducting business with the bank were repeated in another book, and in that book, for the same date, May 19, 1866, Louis Orengo's name is also listed. His place of origin, however, is listed incorrectly as Nowin, Italy. There is no town or region in Italy named Nowin. Perhaps the clerk noted it as some kind of shorthand for northwestern Italy? More likely is that the place Orengo was born, Castel Vittorio, in what is now the Province of Imperia in the region of Liguria, was once not a part of Italy as we know it today. It was part of the Kingdom of Piedmont-Sardinia. It became part of Italy after the Risorgimento in 1861, when Italy was unified. It's possible in 1866, when Orengo told the clerk his place of birth, whether in person or via correspondence, he added, "now in Italy." The "Nowin" is how the clerk noted it. The mistake gives prescient credence to all those immigration stories from later in the century about misspelled names, dropped vowels, and names of towns being erroneously listed as a person's last name.

Why Orengo never sailed for Italy the next day, or if he even intended to, is unclear. Perhaps he had written to the bank in advance, intending to be in New York for his departure, and was unable to travel. What's certain is that he was thinking about his mortality and was concerned about his mother's well-being. Outside of any specific threats to his life or acute health issues, average male life expectancy in 1865 in the United States was only thirty-five years. This was partly due to the Civil War, but even by 1879, it was only thirty-nine years.[6] Orengo was forty-six years old.

In 1867, with the Civil War two years past, railroads stretching across the state, and Orengo no longer tied to the Cathedral in Nashville, he began a breathtakingly productive period of missionary work in Middle and West Tennessee. Once a month, via the Nashville and Northwest Railroad, he attended his home parish St. Patrick's in McEwen more than fifty miles west of Nashville, as well as missions in Newsom Station and Pegram closer to the city. A newspaper reports that finding twenty-five Irish families from counties Kerry and Galway in Bellevue, he organized a mission there. This is likely Newsom Station. The first mass there is believed to have been said by him at Smith's Mill in an old schoolhouse, which is still standing today.[7] The Nashville and Northwest Railroad would also take him up to Union City in Obion County in the northwest corner of the state. It was in 1867 that the first Catholic family arrived in Union City. Hugh Garrigan, the section foreman of the North & Northwest Railroad, offered his home to Fr. Orengo to celebrate mass.[8]

From the Tennessee and Alabama Railroad, Orengo visited Brentwood south of Nashville and five other stations, including Franklin, where on April 12, 1867, he purchased a lot from Julia and Mary Balch for $400.[9] It would be on this property in a few years that the first church in the area would be built.

With access provided by the Nashville and Chattanooga Railroad, Orengo visited missions in Antioch, Murfreesboro and four other locations.

The following two years were no different. Orengo was in McEwen and further west in Humphreys County in Waverly, then south and southeast in Middle Tennessee in Franklin, Johnsonville, Columbia, Camden, Pulaski, Gallatin, Shelbyville, and Tracy City. *The Freeman's Journal*'s correspondent "Charlie," long the admirer of Orengo, took notice. "By exertions of the ever zealous and indefatigable Rev. Louis Orengo who attends to some twenty stations on the line of our three railroads," wrote Charlie on February 6, 1869, "numerous schools have been opened, and in places where a church is scarcely dreamed of at present."[10]

Not everybody was as big of a fan of Orengo's energy and optimism. He was tireless –and being on the fringe of his diocese like Fr.

Samuel Mazzuchelli up in Wisconsin—a bit of a maverick. This rubbed some people the wrong way. Fr. Joseph Augustine Kelly, a Memphis priest, remarked in a diary entry in March of 1868, that Orengo was in Memphis "to build an Italian church, a great humbug that will die still born."[11] Was Kelly admitting some Italian prejudice here? Or did he believe poor Italian immigrants couldn't sustain a church? As Dominican historian Fr. John Vidmar points out, however, Kelly had "underestimated his man."[12] The Italian church of St. Joseph would be founded in Memphis seven years later, with an Italian priest, a Fr. Luisielli, as its first pastor. And then in 1885, St. Lawrence was established in Joelton, Tennessee, by Italian immigrants, with Fr. Orengo's mentee, Fr. Eugene Gazzo, as its first pastor. Orengo was merely laying the groundwork for what was to come.

CHAPTER 10

Jackson, Franklin, Humboldt, and More

Jackson

While some histories erroneously indicate that Fr. Orengo established a short-lived Catholic Church in Jackson, Tennessee, in 1849, there is no doubt that he returned twenty years later and created something far more lasting. Jackson, named after General Andrew Jackson in 1822 to honor his heroics in the War of 1812, is about seventy miles east of Memphis. It's the second largest city in West Tennessee, and by the nineteenth century, had become a major railroad hub in the western part of the state. Madison County records indicate that on March 16, 1869, Orengo made the first-known real estate purchase for the Catholic Church recorded in the city. Bought from Lucy Williams, Jos. N. Williams, and others for $3,000, the purchase included two lots at 109 and 111 North Church Street, where Hub City Bakery and Simpson's Super Stores stood in 1951 (according to a souvenir history published that year of St. Mary's Catholic Church in Jackson).[1] The lots had a combined frontage of 68 feet and depth of 82½ feet. On the property was a 20' × 30' frame carpentry shop consisting of one large and one very small room. The building was immediately remodeled and converted into a Church and was ready for use by midsummer.[2]

Three years later, an adjacent property on Main and Royal in Jackson, known as the Sharpe property, was purchased for a rectory.[3]

Three months after the Church Street property was purchased for the church, the Dominican Sisters of the new St. Agnes Convent in Memphis purchased at auction the nearby twenty-two-acre homestead property of the late General Samuel Jackson Hayes for use as a school.[4]

Among the four teaching Dominican Sisters from St. Agnes in Memphis who came to teach in Jackson were Sister Mary Pius Fitzgerald, Superior, and her biological sister, Sister Vincentia Fitzpatrick. It was at this time that Sister Mary Pius first met Orengo.

"My first acquaintance with him was when we opened a school in Jackson, Tenn. in 1869," she wrote to Diocese of Nashville historian Fr. J. K. Larkin in 1909. "He was our chaplain, often on the road, however, as he had so many outside missions of which you have been informed. The R.R. officials had such respect for him, that he could go here, there and at all times, often accommodating him in the caboose."[5]

Her further description of Orengo's character is among the most vivid portraits of the indefatigable priest.

> As to his personal character, he was, or is one of God's true ministers, following in the footsteps of the Lord; poor, humble, simple and obedient as a child. He never thought of his comfort, many times, tired, hungry and nowhere to lodge, because he did not want to be at a boarding house. He was a missionary for thirty-five years, travelling on foot; on horseback and the R.R. Never a word of odium was cast on him during that time. He stood as one of God's most saintly messengers, and wherever he built a church he drew together the scattered Catholics.
>
> He was a thorough Dominican, which means a great deal, and all his missionary life he never lost the spirit of the true religious.

> His zeal for souls made him forgetful of himself, poor, often needing what was necessary, just so he could live and be able to do his work was all he desired. In his manner he was outspoken and upright to the nicest point, asked no favors. Yet ready to do good for others under all circumstances. Even the bigoted Protestants of Jackson had to admire his zeal and activity, though in his sermons he never spared them.
>
> I cannot give you a fair estimate of his worth. A faithful servant, and zealous priest and true religious sums up his character.

Pulaski

On one of his many missionary trips, which now took slightly less time with the advent of the railroad, Orengo might have taken the railroad north from Jackson and switched to the Louisville & Nashville railroad briefly before catching the Nashville & Chattanooga line at McKenzie east to Nashville, where he would have gotten on a southbound Louisville & Nashville train to take him to Pulaski, Tennessee. For it was there in 1871, about 130 miles as the crow flies from Jackson, that Orengo erected his next church, near the railroad for its convenience. The Pulaski faithful acquired a lot, about 200 square feet, from a prominent merchant named Thomas Martin at a cost of $200, upon which they put up a building 30' × 40'. It was a frame structure of box type on a rock foundation that was eventually fortified with brick.[6] The church was christened St. Augustine. Orengo came once a month to celebrate mass.[7]

Franklin

Orengo's next two parishes had him back and forth between Middle and West Tennessee on those same railroad lines. First came Franklin in 1871, when he oversaw the building of St. Philip Catholic Church on the property first purchased in 1867.

The dedication of St. Philip on November 6, 1871, presided over by Bishop Patrick Richard Feehan with Orengo as resident mission priest, was a celebratory affair. A special train comprising eight cars left at 8:45 A.M. from the Nashville and Decatur Depot, located on the corner of Chestnut Street and Cherry Street (now 4th Avenue South), to take Catholics from Nashville to Franklin. Several societies joined in the procession, meeting up at the depot as early as 7:30 A.M. Among them were the St. Joseph's Total Abstinence Society and band, followed by the St. Mary's Sanctuary Society, the Society of St. Vincent de Paul, St. Mary's Orphan Association, and finally, the Hibernia Society. Following the dedication, Bishop Feehan celebrated mass. In his homily, he preached from 1 Kings 9:3: "The Lord said to him: I have heard the prayer of petition which you offered in my presence. I have consecrated this house which you have built and set my name there forever; my eyes and my heart shall be there always."[8]

The service ended at 1 P.M., and revelers spilled out into the town. "Franklin was ransacked for dinners," reported the *Nashville Union and American*.[9]

St. Philip's, which remained a mission church until 1897, when it was declared a parish and Fr. John A. Nolan its first pastor, still stands and thrives today. Under the leadership of now-retired pastor Fr. Ed Steiner, membership at the church soared to more than four thousand parishioners by 2023, due in part to exponential growth in Williamson County. Fr. Steiner has a unique connection to the parish's history. Original pastor Fr. Nolan's Irish grandparents, John Nowlin and Margaret Alyward, are Steiner's great-great-great-grandparents, The parish has outgrown its confines multiple times over its history, and thanks either to the frugality of its parishioners, or a preservationist mindset, church leadership built upon existing structures

FIGURE 10.1. A Williamson County Historical Society historical marker in Franklin, Tennessee, recognizing the role of Fr. Orengo as a missionary priest and in the establishment of St. Philip Catholic Church. Photo courtesy of the author.

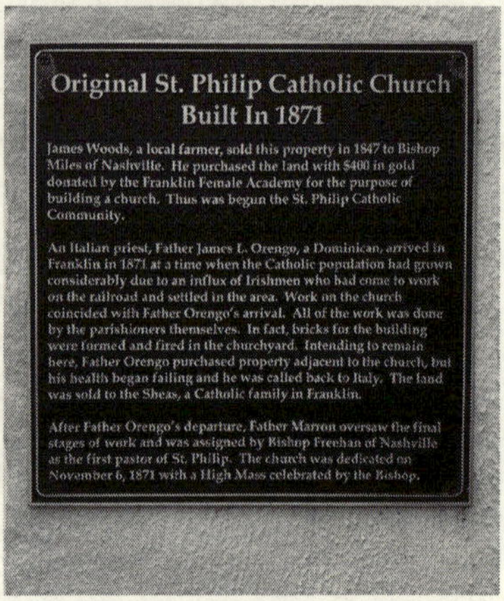

FIGURE 10.2. A marker near the door of the original St. Philip Catholic Church, now the chapel in Franklin, Tennessee, recognizing Fr. Orengo's role in establishing it in 1871. Photo courtesy of the author.

instead of knocking them down. The original 1871 church is now the church's chapel, and the only extant structure you can visit today that was built and touched by Orengo's hands.

During a visit to the church in 2024, Kim Leisinger, who among her many duties at the church manages its bookstore, let me into the original chapel. It's still occasionally used for small services and weddings. It's been remarkably cared for by the parish. Not long ago during a renovation, its flooring was removed to reveal its original subfloor. Leisinger left me alone for a little while, to run my fingers along the chapel's brick walls, say a prayer, and try as I might to feel Orengo's presence. I knew that he was getting to the end of his journey in Tennessee when he built the church, which meant that I was getting to the end of my journey, too. We had some notes to compare.

FIGURE 10.3. The original St. Philip Catholic Church, now a chapel, in Franklin, Tennessee. Photo courtesy of the author.

FIGURE 10.4. The nave and sanctuary of the original St. Philip Catholic Church, now a chapel, in Franklin, Tennessee. Photo courtesy of the author.

Humboldt

Following the dedication of St. Philip, Orengo was back in West Tennessee. In 1872, he oversaw the building of a wood church in Humboldt christened St. Louis. The land on which the church was built was donated by the Donovan family, along with adequate space for a rectory and school.[10]

While there were Catholic families in the town who offered hospitality to Orengo on his mission visits, he chose instead to stay in a little room at the back of the church where he cooked his humble meals with whatever provisions he could gather, usually pasta, cheese, crackers, bread and olive oil.

Orengo appeared to find affection and make great friends everywhere he went, but he seemed to make lifelong friends in Humboldt. It was there that he met the Russells: saloon keeper Thomas (age 39 in the 1870 census) and his wife Mary (age 35), both born in Ireland. They had three children: Jennie (age 12), Lawrence (age 7) and Johnnie (age 4). They appear to have migrated to Tennessee in the mid-to-late 1860s, as Jennie and Lawrence are both listed as being born in Iowa, and Johnnie as being born in Gibson County, Tennessee. They had another child in 1871, Molly. Orengo exchanged letters with Jennie and Johnnie in the mid-to-late 1880s after he returned to Italy. In the letters, Orengo expresses great affection for the Russells, while also asking about other residents of Humboldt and nearby Brownsville he had come to know well. This included a Captain McMullen, who was the brother of the late John McMullen, bishop of Davenport, Iowa, who died in 1883, and a Mrs. Kelly in Brownsville, whose son appears to have been a "rude and incorrigible fellow" according to Orengo. To Johnnie in 1885, he asks about Jennie, "For I loved her and all of you as my best friends when I was in Humboldt, and often think of you all and pray for you and your good father." In a letter to Jennie in 1888, he writes that "my very best friends were your good parents

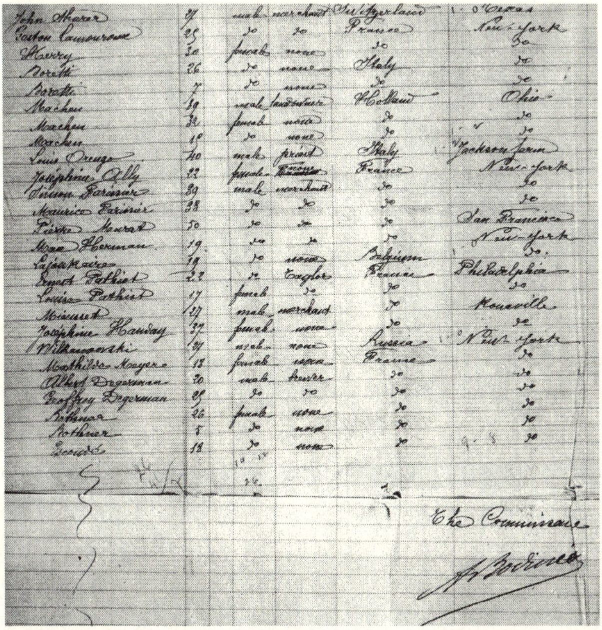

FIGURE 10.5. Fr. Orengo returned to New York City from Europe on the ship *Washington* on December 10, 1872. His occupation is listed as "priest" and his destination "Jackson Farm."

whilst I was in Humboldt. I every day pray for you in my Mass that God may keep you under his special protection and grace."[11] Jennie had sent Orengo photos of her and her siblings, and Orengo notes the changes in their appearance, as it's been more than a decade and a half since he has seen them. "Thank you very heartily for sending me your picture," he wrote, "together with Molly's and Laurence's [*sic*], which I kissed many times and keep it carefully. Yours is very returned to me. Laurence too is natural, but it seems not very correct. Molly's I did not recognize well as I left her very small but she is a very fine little child God bless her."[12] When Orengo learns of the passing of Johnnie and Jennie's mother, Mary, he tells Jennie that "I feel very much for you . . . orphaned children . . . you have a hard life my friend Jennie but God will help you; work together and be united . . . Fear God, and be devout of the B.V. [Blessed Virgin] Mary."[13]

In addition to admonitions to both Jennie and Johnnie to be good Catholics and attend to their churches, go to confession, "keep away from bad company," and pray for him, Orengo also expresses longing for his mission in Humboldt, and missions elsewhere in Tennessee, which he feels are going into disrepair since his departure. "I wish I could be with you in Humboldt," he wrote to Johnnie in 1885, "and repair and serve your little church, but I am 65 years old and of little use in America. I am sorry that my little churches are going to nothing."[14] That same year, in an additional letter to Johnnie, Orengo wrote, "When you write to me again I like to know more about the Catholics of Humboldt, Brownsville and Grand Junction and how (they) are carrying on their church, if they have a Priest attending to them at least occasionally. My other missions in Middle Tennessee, Columbia, Pulaski, Franklin, and Gallatin I fear are also neglected."

Orengo is forlorn in the letters, resigned to the idea that what he created in Tennessee might not last. It's heartbreaking to read, as time would eventually prove him wrong. But at the time, he was being pragmatic. Catholics at the time were typically poor laborers. To sustain even a modest parish, there needs to be available work. "There is no right emigration to Tennessee," he writes. "Except Memphis and Nashville other places in Tennessee offer poor encouragement for Catholics. The negros are the laborers there."[15]

Later in the year after establishing the mission in Humboldt, Orengo appears to have at some point traveled again to Europe and arrived back in the United States on December 10, 1872, on the French steamer ship *Washington* from the port of Le Havre, France. His occupation is listed as "priest" and home country as Italy. The place listed on the ship manifest where he plans to reside is noted as "Jackson Farm."[16] Like in McEwen, he had clearly found a home in Madison County.

CHAPTER 11

Yellow Fever, Cholera, and a Return to Italy

> I offer every step for some missionary who, far away, is exhausted by his work for souls; I offer my exhaustion for his.
> —St. Therese of Lisieux

While the yellow fever epidemic in Memphis in 1855 was deadly, the 1873 yellow fever outbreak, coupled with an outbreak of cholera, was devastating to the city and West Tennessee. Fevers were widespread throughout, and thousands of citizens trying to flee the disease took the carrier mosquito with them to towns east and north of the city, including Collierville, Paris, Brownsville, Milan, and Martin. Their fear was warranted. During the combined epidemics of 1873 and 1878, more than seven thousand Memphis residents who stayed behind died.[1] Cholera made things worse in Memphis, but even more so in Nashville. *The New York Times* of July 11, 1873, reported that there was "Filth enough in Nashville and Memphis to give the scourge a strong foothold."

> From Memphis to Nashville the disease seemed to jump at one spring. The capital city was evidently in a frightful sanitary condition. The city is built on a huge limestone rock. Its drainage

> and sewerage is all on the surface. Its streets are narrow, and the city is compactly built. It has a large idle population, whose habits of living are not of the best. It has a large part of this population gathered in flats and along some sluggish creeks, into which empties what little of sewerage the city has. In these flats are two springs, out of which the poor people take their water. The experience during the epidemic has demonstrated that this water acted like poison. It was almost certain to produce cholera whenever used.[2]

Deaths from cholera in Nashville at the time of the article were estimated at eight hundred. Gallatin, Shelbyville, Clarksville, Murfreesboro, Franklin, Pulaski, and McMinnville all experienced devastating losses of its citizens. Many of the towns in Middle and West Tennessee were places Orengo had established missions and churches and often visited. The double scourge of yellow fever and cholera proved too much for the indefatigable servant.

In a letter dated October 24, 1873, to Father Raymond Bianchi in Kentucky—he was still ultimately taking his orders from the Dominican Province of St. Joseph—Orengo wrote to ask to retire from the missions:

> Dear Father, in these missions we were very afflicted for 8 months. 1. Spring the smallpox that caused much slaughter 2. Summer the cholera that carried away miles. Now, autumns [*sic*], since September 3rd we have yellow fever, terrible fever. Four of our Dominican Fathers from Memphis Tennessee, Fr. [George Raymond] Daily [Dailey], Fr. Bartholomew Vincent Carey, Fr. [Denis Augustin] O'Brien, and Fr. John [Dominic] Sheehy died in 3 weeks. Now the Prior Fr. [Joseph Augustine] has the yellow blacksmith.

FIGURE 11.1. Portrait of Fr. Orengo in Nashville in the early 1870s, prior to the end of his missions in Tennessee. The cabinet card was likely reprinted years later by Reeves photography studio from a negative of a photo taken by another studio, as Reeves did not set up shop in Nashville until the late 1880s.

His request was granted. Before Orengo's departure in 1873 from Tennessee, Orengo married several couples at his beloved St. Patrick's Church, the last recorded being that of Mike Tarpy and Mary Herity, ancestors of Barbara Hooper, and the grandparents of the boy who would grow up to be Fr. Joseph Tarpy, one of St. Patrick's early pastors.

On November 20, 1873, Orengo returned to St. Rose Convent in Washington County, Kentucky, from where he departed twenty-five years earlier for Tennessee. Though the friars gave him a warm welcome, he was undecided at first whether he should end his days at

St. Rose or go back to Italy. Fr. Hugh Francis Lilly, prior of St. Rose Convent at the time, felt that the aged missionary would be more "at home" with the "brethren of his own blood, and rather advised him to go to them."[3]

Orengo sailed for his home country around Christmas of 1873.

CHAPTER 12

Final Years in Italy

Orengo returned to Italy, as he told Johnnie Russell in Humboldt in a letter years later, to cure what was then known as rheumatism. He wanted to go back to America after his health returned, but his Superior General wouldn't consent to it. He first went to his home region, the town of Taggia in the Province of Imperia in the region of Liguria, where he founded an orphanage that was still in existence into the mid-1920s. By the spring of 1877, his activities in the area made news back in Kentucky. The *Lexington Herald*, and subsequently the *Maysville Bulletin* and *Republican*, reported that "Father Louis Orengo, who was once pastor of St. Dominico church at Springfield, and who established seven or eight missions in Tennessee, has purchased a place on the Mediterranean sea, containing a stone house built in the middle ages, and will organize an asylum for the exiled Dominican fathers."[1] Orengo found time to break from his work on December 29, 1877, when he went to the Taggia office of John Baptist Curlo to testify and sign a quit claim to the church in Jackson. He still owned the deed. All rights were transferred to Bishop Patrick Feehan, "for the use and benefit of the Catholic Church in the City of Jackson, County of Madison State of Tennessee." The written testimony and signature were mailed to Jackson and entered into the record in Madison County by register of deeds J. M. Hardage on February 18, 1878.

Orengo left Liguria in 1879 to live for a year and act as sub-prior of a Dominican convent in Civitavecchia, on the coast of the Tyrrhenian Sea west of Rome. He visited Rome several times while there, but it broke his heart. He wrote to Johnnie Russell: "I would see the King Humberto in the Palace of the Pope, with his officials and troops of robbers round him . . . the poor Pope shut up in the Vatican Palace at St. Peter's . . . the Catholic Religion and the monks and nuns persecuted, driven out of their convents on the cold world."

In the late 1870s, King Umberto I, successor to King Emmanuele II of the House of Savoy, began his very complicated relationship with the Catholic Church. After Umberto's march into Rome, division between the House of Savoy and the Vatican remained unresolved until Umberto's assassination in 1900.[2]

In 1880, Orengo returned to Imperia, where for a time he lived an austere and eremitic life, very much alone, just outside of Taggia. The Dominican Convent of Taggia at the time was inhabited by the Friars of the Province of St. Peter the Martyr of Piedmont. At Easter time, Orengo would travel to the convent to help with the influx of Catholics seeking the sacrament of confession.

In late 1883, he went for a brief time to serve in the Alps, but the weather was cold and challenging. He returned on December 11, 1884, to Imperia and the seaside town of Sanremo, where he lived among people, mostly all Catholic, whom he described as poor and oppressed.

"The women work as hard as the men on the land," Orengo wrote. "They are very brown, almost like the melatonin of America. They dress very poorly; they are a very pitiful sect of people, generally ignorant in letters but knowing their religion well as whole; they are very devout of the Blessed Virgin; they are very awfully oppressed with taxes by the government, the province and the town, they never can have a cent."

It is there, it appears, Orengo finally got some relief for his rheumatism and a brief respite from his life of labor. The poor people treated him well, offering him beans and fruit and figs and wine. Half a mile from Sanremo, "in a grove of olive trees, lemons, figs and wine grapes," he lived in a small sanctuary—"as big as your bedroom" he told Johnnie Russell—dedicated to Mary. It was called by the locals the sanctuary of la Madonna della Misericordia del Borgo, after a painting housed within it of the Blessed Mother.

> It is a painting on a pillar of a door of a garden and being very miraculous the proprietor built over it a small chapel and a sacristy and over it a room for a chaplain. The people here are very fervent toward this very miraculous image of the Mother of God. The proprietor invited me to stay in it and officiate in it. I live in it like a hermit. I am alone. The proprietor gives me one dollar a week and on Sunday the mass is celebrated. The image is life size and painted on slate, very old. Years ago the colors of her face, hands and dress being very much faded, it was repaired and in a very short time the new colors left it and it is now as it was centuries ago. The walls of the little church are literally covered with . . . donations of little pictures of graces conferred on those devout sick or most needy that have had their recourse. To her with sincerity I too have experienced her intercession. When I got here I was very sick for three weeks and full of rheumatism. I recommended myself to this most holy Mother and am now very well. I never saw a picture that inspires me more with contrition for my sins and confidence in God's mercy than this.

With his health restored, Orengo returned to Taggia and was back to his indefatigable self as best he could, traveling around the Ligurian province as needed. He encouraged and advised the youth in San Luigi, about fifty kilometers north of Taggia, to build a church in the town, and carried the stones himself. "Having no home, he lived in a hut, where no ordinary animal would have lived," wrote Don

Giovanni Nicora of Castel Vittorio to Fr. Victor O'Daniel in April 11, 1926. "Where in one corner he lit a fire; he had put a pot for eating, which was polenta or cornmeal or chestnut; and the door never closed while he asked the youth to transport the stones."

"(He was a) True model of obedience," added Nicora. "Words are insufficient to praise that man of God."

By the end of 1885, Orengo was celebrating two masses every Sunday in two churches half an hour away from each other, one named in honor of St. John the Baptist, and another St. James the Apostle, both one hour from Sanremo and three hours from Taggia.

By 1888, Orengo had taken up residence at the Ospedale Civile Mauriziano in Sanremo—the Mauriziano Hospital—a former leprosarium that had earlier that decade been transferred to the municipality to become a civic hospital that continued to care for those with leprosy as needed.[3]

Even though he was building orphanages and chapels and caring for the poor and sick in northern Italy, Orengo continued to request and receive news from Tennessee. A Miss Mary McQuire of Nashville (Mrs. Byrne in 1885) regularly sent him the *Nashville American*. He repaid her by saying masses for her mother and father. He also subscribed to *The Freeman's Journal* for several years and paid for the service by saying twelve masses a year for editor James Alphonsus McMaster. When he moved to Sanremo, where he ministered to the poor farmers and said fewer masses than before, he offered to say four masses for McMaster, after which the paper stopped coming.[4]

"If you could occasionally send me some Catholic newspaper which you may get from Catholic friends or peddlers, even the *Irish World*, I would be very thankful to you," Orengo wrote Johnnie Russell in 1885.[5]

In 1891, Orengo moved to the Roman Province and the town of Viterbo, where he lived in a small alley apartment with a succession of other friars, close to the Monastery of San Domenico in Viterbo.

He acted as the confessor of the Dominican Sisters of the Monasteries of Saint Catherine VM, a role he exercised until 1899.

Orengo eventually retired to the Dominican Convent at the Basilica of Santa Maria della Quercia in Viterbo. He was going blind and needed nearly round-the-clock care. When celebrating mass, he often needed assistance placing the consecrated host in the monstrance. Fr. Paul-Marie Girardin, Chaplain of the Dominicans of Marin and a professor at the College of La Quercia, was his nurse for five years. In a letter to Fr. O'Daniel in 1926, Girardin said Orengo celebrated a votive mass every day in honor of the Blessed Mother, until paralysis confined him to his bed.[6] His memory remained intact, however, and he talked willingly of his missions in Tennessee. His infirmities "took nothing away from his serenity," wrote Girardin. "He even joked willingly."

One of his favorite things to joke about when it came to his missions in Tennessee was that he did not wear his full habit when riding a horse. "Ma, sa, io aveva il permesso!" he would exclaim. But, you know, I had permission!

On March 18, 1909, on the day after The Feast of St. Patrick and the evening before the Solemnity of St. Joseph, in the presence of the entire community, Orengo received the last sacraments from the hands of the Father Prior, Father Novaro. Around 10 P.M., he died without agony, in full consciousness, repeating the prayer of the good thief, which was his favorite prayer: "Domine, memento mei. Domine, miserere mei." Lord, remember me. Lord have mercy on me.

Epilogue

Before leaving Tennessee, Fr. Orengo gave to Fr. Eugene Gazzo, his mentee and fellow Italian Dominican Friar, his copy of Jesuit priest Joanne Petro Gury's *Compendium Theologiae Moralis* (*Moral Theology*) on which he had written the closest thing we have to his résumé. He wrote his name as Fr. Aloysius Orengo, OP, and then in Latin wrote that he came from St. Rose in Kentucky to serve Most Rev. Richard Pius Miles in Nashville. On the fly leaf of the book, he noted that he had built churches in Franklin, Columbia, Pulaski, Edgefield Junction, Tracy City, Gallatin, Humboldt, Brownsville, Grand Junction, and Covington, and that he had extracted the churches at Jackson, Shelbyville, and Clarksville from much debt. He purchased land for churches in Fayetteville, Lincoln Co., Trenton, Gibson Co., Union City, and Jackson. He ended by writing that he founded the colony at McEwen, Humphreys Co. on March 27, 1848.[1] He closed in English, "Remember me, poor sinner, in your prayers."

As of this writing, most of the communities Fr. Orengo noted on his *Moral Theology* still have a Catholic Church, even if the physical building, location, and makeup of the congregations have changed. In 2024, there were 106 parishes in Middle and West Tennessee, serving 146,000 Catholics. Many are thriving today with a mix of native

Tennesseans, transplants from around the country, and like the Irish in the mid-to-late nineteenth century, a new wave of immigrants, this time mostly from Mexico and Central America, who have breathed new life into the faith and their communities. Orengo's impact can be felt even in communities where he did not establish churches. In 1948, Bishop William Adrian of the Diocese of Nashville named the area of Camden, Tennessee, a mission to be served by St. Patrick's in McEwen. It became a parish, St. Mary's, in 1981 under the Diocese of Memphis.

In 2010, the Williamson County Historical Society erected a plaque in front of St. Philip Catholic Church at East Main Street and 2nd Ave in Franklin noting that "Until 1898 the church had mission status with Father James Orengo of Italy as the first mission priest." In 2020, the Tennessee Historical Commission, through the encouragement and enthusiasm of Ted Rice at the Humphreys County Museum and Civil War Fort, placed a marker in front of St. Patrick's Church and School in McEwen. It states, "In 1849, Father Aloysius Orengo built a small log church near here to serve the Irish immigrants who were sheep herders and furnace workers. Six years later, in 1855 he moved the log church to this site and established Humphreys County's first school. To raise funds for a bell, Father Orengo sponsored the first Irish Picnic that is now an annual event in McEwen." The Irish Picnic at St. Patrick's in McEwen, considering 1854 its first year, celebrated its 170th anniversary in 2024.

It was one hundred years ago as of this writing that Fr. Victor F. O'Daniel wrote "We have heard more than one regret that [Fr. Orengo's] life has not been written, for it would make a story of intense interest."[2]

One hundred years later, I hope I have written Fr. Orengo's life well and turned some of that regret into contentment.

NOTES

PREFACE

1. V. F. O'Daniel and James Reginald Coffey, *The First Two Dominican Priories in the United States: Saint Rose's Priory, Near Springfield, KY; Saint Joseph's Priory, Somerset, OH* (Holy Name Society, 1947), 79.

2. V. F. O'Daniel, *The Father of the Church in Tennessee; or, The Life, Times, and Character of the Right Reverend Richard Pius Miles, O.P., the First Bishop of Nashville* (Dominicana, 1926),. 563.

3. V. F. O'Daniel, *The Right Rev. Edward Dominic Fenwick, O.P., Founder of the Dominicans in the United States, Pioneer Missionary in Kentucky, Apostle of Ohio, First Bishop of Cincinnati* (Dominicana, 1920), 4.

4. Fr. Samuel Mazzuchelli's 1844 memoir, as we will see, is an exception to this rule.

5. James T. Keane, *Reading Culture Through Catholic Eyes: 50 Writers, Thinkers & Firebrands Who Challenge & Change Us* (Orbis Books, 2024), 28.

INTRODUCTION

1. You'll have to watch the episode to see why Miss Amy is faking her own death, and how it all shakes out.

2. *Freeman's Journal*, February 6, 1869; *Nashville Union and American*, April 16, 1870.

3. V. F. O'Daniel notes, from the Orengo files in the archives at Eastern Province of Dominicans in Washington, DC (hereafter, Orengo files).

4. V. F. O'Daniel notes, Orengo files.

5. C. W. Russell, "Letter to John Larkin, April 16, 1910," Orengo files.

6. Sacramental evidence from archives at the Diocese of Nashville.

7. F. Gavin Davenport, *Cultural Life in Nashville on the Eve of the Civil War* (University of North Carolina Press, 1941), 84.

8. Davenport, *Cultural Life in Nashville*, 94.

9. Davenport, *Cultural Life in Nashville*, 108.

10. V. F. O'Daniel notes, Orengo files.

11. John Higham, *Strangers in the Land: Patterns of American Nativism, 1860–1925* (Atheneum, 1965), 5.

12. Rev. Edward J. Kuettner, "Letter: to Rev. John K. Larkin, July 7, 1909." Archives at St. Patrick's Church in McEwen.

13. Fr. Eugene Gazzo, OP, a successor and mentee of Orengo, told this story in an interview in October 1924 with Fr. V. F. O'Daniel, as archived in the Orengo files at the Eastern Province Archives of the Dominicans in Washington, DC: "On one occasion some of the high-browed ladies complained to the bishop that Father Orengo did not preach clearly, and that his English was not good. The complaint finally reached Father Orengo's ears. The next time he preached, he spoke on all the Ten Commandments, closing his remarks on each with: 'If you do this,' or 'If you don't do this,' as the subject demanded, 'You will go to Hell. Do you understand me? Do I speak plain English?' There were no more complaints."

14. Fr. Luigi Orengo, "Letter: to Johnnie Russell, April 16, 1885." Orengo files.

15. Orengo, "Letter: to Johnnie Russell," Orengo files.

16. "Nobody worked as long, as hard, and as productively as Father Orengo," wrote Thomas Stritch in his 1987 history, *The Catholic Church in Tennessee.* "His labors were Herculean. He went everywhere, knew everybody, and everybody seemed to know him. His accomplishments were outstanding." Thomas Stritch, *The Catholic Church in Tennessee: The Sesquicentennial Story* (Catholic Center, 1987).

CHAPTER 1

1. "Orengo," Wikipedia, Italian edition, last modified June 11, 2025, 11:09 (UTC), https://it.wikipedia.org/w/index.php?title=Orengo.

2. "Lorenzo Orengo - Restoration Completed: Memorials to Benjamin Whitehead and Julia Morison Bentley, 1885 and 1887, Restored in 2013," American Friends of Italian Monumental Sculpture: Camposanto di Staglieno, Genoa, Italy, https://staglieno.com/Orengo-Whitehead.html.

3. Mary Joan Leith, "The Crucifixion Conundrum and the Santa Sabina Doors." *Harvard Theological Review* 103, no. 1 (2010), 67.

4. V. F. O'Daniel, *The Dominican Province of Saint Joseph, Historico-Biographical Studies* (Holy Name Society, 1942), 178.

5. O'Daniel, *The Father of the Church*.

6. O'Daniel, *The Father of the Church*.

7. Stritch, *The Catholic Church*.

8. Letters from Girardin to O'Daniel, March 20, 1926, Orengo files.

9. "Henri Lacordaire," *Encyclopedia Britannica*, last updated Nov. 17, 2025, https://www.britannica.com/biography/Henri-Lacordaire.

10. Samuel Mazzuchelli, *The Memoirs of Father Samuel Mazzuchelli* (Priory Press, 1967).

11. Cabrini was canonized in 1946.

12. "New York, Passenger Lists, 1820–1920," entry for Louis Orengo, 1845, FamilySearch, https://www.familysearch.org/ark:/61903/1:1:QVPF-765V.

13. Paul M. Starrs, "The California Chronicle of Francis Sadoc Vilarrasa, OP, 1850–1874." *Catholic Historical Review* 37, no. 4 (Jan. 1952): 415–36.

14. "History - St. Rose Priory Church, Springfield, Kentucky," St. Rose Priory Church, October 30, 2024, https://strosespringfield.org/about/history/.

15. "Eugene Magevney Historical Marker," Historical Marker Database, February 7, 2023, https://www.hmdb.org/m.asp?m=32518.

16. "History of St. Dominic Catholic Church," Saint Dominic Catholic Church, http://stdomparish.org.

17. Victor O'Daniel notes, Orengo files.

18. Victor O'Daniel notes, Orengo files.

19. O'Daniel, *The Father of the Church.*

20. Mary Nona McGreal, *The Order of Preachers in the United States: A Family History*, vol. 1, *Dominicans at Home in a Young Nation: 1786–1865* (Editions du Signe, 2001), chapter 8.

CHAPTER 2

1. Thomas H. Winn, "Clarksville," Tennessee Encyclopedia, last updated March 1, 2018, https://tennesseeencyclopedia.net/entries/clarksville/.

2. Susan Douglas Wilson, "Transportation in Early Middle Tennessee," *Middle Tennessee Genealogy* 7, no. 4 (Spring 1994): 148–52. Reprinted on Rootsweb, https://sites.rootsweb.com/~tnsumner/mdtntran.htm.

3. Wilson, "Transportation in Early Middle Tennessee."

4. Bill Carey, "Ridesharing . . . 1800s Style," *Tennessee Magazine*, November 1, 2022, https://www.tnmagazine.org/ridesharing-1800s-style/.

5. Kristen A Bradley, "A Tennessee Irish Picnic: Foodways and Complex Community Dynamics" (PhD diss., University of Louisiana at Lafayette, 2014), 20.

6. Bradley, "A Tennessee Irish Picnic."

7. Stritch, *The Catholic Church.*

8. Bradley, "A Tennessee Irish Picnic."

9. *The Catholic Almanac for 1848* (F. Lucas, Jr., Baltimore, 1848).

10. Bradley, "A Tennessee Irish Picnic."

11. Bradley, "A Tennessee Irish Picnic."

12. Bradley, "A Tennessee Irish Picnic."

13. O'Daniel, *The Father of the Church*, 402.

14. *The Catholic Almanac for 1848* (F. Lucas, Jr., Baltimore, 1848).

15. Michael Gavin, *Tennessee Iron Furnace Trail: A Guide to Resources on the Western Highland Rim*, illus. Barry Graham (Center for Historic Preservation, Middle Tennessee State University, 2006).

16. *The Catholic Almanac for 1849* (F. Lucas, Jr., Baltimore, 1849).

17. Joel William McGraw et al., *Between the Rivers: The Catholic Heritage of West Tennessee* (Catholic Diocese of Memphis; J.S. Sanders & Co, 1996), 36.

18. O'Daniel, *The Father of the Church*, 428.

19. A law required mail left at the post office be advertised in the local paper.

20. Sacramental records from the archives at the Diocese of Nashville.

21. United States Work Projects Administration. "Interview: Emma Grisham," in *Tennessee Narratives*, vol. 15 of *Slave Narratives: A Folk History of Slavery in the United States from Interviews with Former Slaves* (Library of Congress Project, WPA, 2006).

22. Regarding the Roman Catholic Church's position on slavery: In the centuries prior to the nineteenth, the Church certainly embraced slavery, authorized the slave trade and permitted Catholics to keep enslaved persons. Progress was made slowly. While in 1839, Pope Gregory XVI condemned the slave trade, he did not indicate whether slaveholders in America should free their enslaved people. In 1864, the Vatican condemned slavery as being incompatible with Christianity, but the decision was never made public. The 1866 Plenary Council of Baltimore spoke often of slavery but made no decisive plan of action as to what to do about it. It wasn't until 1888 that Pope Leo XIII formally changed the church's teaching and publicly opposed slavery. In the case of Tennessee, Bishop Miles made no public pronouncement on slavery.

23. Kenneth Feith, "Cumberland Compact," Tennessee Encyclopedia, last updated March 1, 2018, http://tennesseeencyclopedia.net/entries/cumberland-compact/.

24. *Nashville Union and American*, January 11, 1873.

25. Elizabeth Elkins, *We Should Soon Become Respectable: Nashville's Own Timothy Demonbreun* (Vanderbilt University Press, 2022), 78.

CHAPTER 3

1. *The Tennessee Register*, May 15, 1949.

2. John Lehman, "Letter to Fr. George Flanigen, Feb. 10, 1967." The Flanigen Papers archive at Aquinas College Library.

3. *The Tennessean*, October 23, 1905.

4. *The Tennessean*, October 23, 1905.

5. Mazzuchelli, *Memoirs*, vii.

6. Eliza Pyburn, "The Parish of McEwen, Tennessee," March 31–April 2, 1909, from the archives at St. Patrick's Church in McEwen, Tennessee.

7. *Shanks mare* means "on his own two feet." Euchre is a trick-taking card game that was popular at the time in the Midwest United States

8. Conversation with O'Daniel and Gazzo, October 1924, from Orengo files.

9. *Nashville Daily American*, January 9, 1882.

10. Mary Cabrini Durkin and Mary Nona McGreal, *Always on Call: Samuel Mazzuchelli of the Order of Preachers, 1806–1864* (Éditions du Signe, 2000), 18.

11. Durkin and McGreal, *Always on Call*, 18.

12. Davenport, *Cultural Life in Nashville*, 94

13. Higham, *Strangers in the Land*, 6.

14. Davenport, *Cultural Life in Nashville*, 108.

15. Higham, *Strangers in the Land*, 6.

16. Sydney E. Ahlstrom, *A Religious History of the American People*, vol. 1 (Image Books, 1975), 676–81.

17. Paul Heller, "Montpelier's Secret Society: The Order of the Star-Spangled Banner," *Times Argus*, August 6, 2024. https://www.timesargus.com/news/local/montpelier-s-secret-society-the-order-of-the-star-spangled-banner/article_29d9fa06-5105-11ef-a4c2-f71686ad5734.html.

18. Heller, "Montpelier's Secret Society."

19. Msgr. Owen Campion, "Andrew Johnson: Remembering a Champion of the Church," *Our Sunday Visitor*, January 17, 2020. https://www.oursundayvisitor.com/andrew-johnson-remembering-a-champion-of-the-church/.

20. Betsey Johnson, "Looking Back, Mercy in a Time of Fear," SistersofMercy.org, January 8, 2018, https://www.sistersofmercy.org/looking-back-mercy-in-a-time-of-fear/.

21. O'Daniel, *The Father of the Church*, 523–24.

22. *Brownlow's Knoxville Whig*, March 10, 1855; see also Laurence V. Gibney Jr., *The Church on Summit Hill: The Catholics of Knoxville and East Tennessee* (Immaculate Conception Church, 1986) *Journal of East Tennessee Historical Society*, March 1980.

23. Higham, *Strangers in the Land*, 7.

24. Sister Aloysius Mackin, OP, *To Others: Sketches of a Catholic Educator in Tennessee, 1860–1921* (St. Cecilia Congregation, 1991), 19.

25. Davenport, *Cultural Life in Nashville*, 109.

CHAPTER 4

1. Jerry T. Wooten, *Johnsonville: Union Supply Operations on the Tennessee River and the Battle of Johnsonville, November 4–5, 1864* (Savas Beatie, 2021), 23.

2. Bradley, "A Tennessee Irish Picnic."

3. Eliza Pyburn, "The Parish of McEwen, Tennessee." March 31–April 2, 1909, from the archives at St. Patrick's Church in McEwen, Tennessee.

4. "Guinness Book of Records: World Record," July 25, 1986, available at "A Community Tradition," St. Patrick's Irish Picnic, https://irishpicnic.com/history/.

5. Bradley, "A Tennessee Irish Picnic."

6. *The Metropolitan Catholic Almanac and Laity's Directory for the Year of Our Lord 1856* (Lucas Brothers, Baltimore, 1856).

7. Mary Catherine Strobel was murdered outside a department store in downtown Nashville in 1986 after being kidnapped by an escaped convict. Fr. Charles Strobel and his family publicly forgave the killer and later petitioned the district attorney to not seek the death penalty. For more about Fr. Charles Stronbel, see his posthumous memoir, *The Kingdom of the Poor: My Journey Home* (Vanderbilt University Press, 2024).

CHAPTER 5

1. *The Daily Appeal* of Memphis, September 18, 1855.

2. Christopher Caplinger, "Yellow Fever Epidemics," *Tennessee Encyclopedia*, last updated March 1, 2018. https://tennesseeencyclopedia.net/entries/yellow-fever-epidemics/.

3. Father of the Waters refers to the Mississippi River.

4. *Memphis Daily Avalanche*, Sunday, July 10, 1887.

5. Among these churches are several in the author's hometown of Jersey City, New Jersey.

6. The transept is the area of a cruciform, or cross-shaped church, that juts out to the left and right of the main axis of the church at right angles, creating the appearance of a cross in the nave.

7. *Memphis Daily Appeal*, July 12, 1859.

8. Cornelia Jean Crowley O'Connor, *Immaculate Conception Church: Its History, Its People* (Immaculate Conception Church, Clarksville, TN, 1980).

9. "History," Immaculate Conception Catholic Church and School, Clarksville, TN, Immachttps://immaconception.org/history.

10. "Schedule 1. Free Inhabitants in 6th Civil District in the County of Humphreys State of Tennessee," page no. 67, United States, Census, 1860—Population, National Archives and Records Administration, microfilm publication M653, via FamilySearch, https://www.familysearch.org/ark:/61903/3:1:33S7-9BS6-QLK?wc=7QMS-Z35%3A1589422383%2C1589436299%2C1589436012%26cc%3D1473181&cc=1473181&lang=en&i=4.

CHAPTER 6

1. *London Guardian*, June 4, 1859.
2. *Daily Nashville Patriot*, February 22, 1860.
3. *Republican Banner*, Nashville, February 23, 1860.
4. Davenport, *Cultural Life in Nashville*, 111.

CHAPTER 7

1. TN Civil War GIS project, https://tnmap.tn.gov/civilwar.
2. Wooten, *Johnsonville*, 30.
3. Wooten, *Johnsonville*, 31.
4. A generic term for a pocket pistol.
5. C.W. Russell, "Letter to John Larkin, April 16, 1910." Orengo files.
6. "Page 11 - US, Southern Claims Commission Approved Claims, 1871–1880," Fold3, https://www.fold3.com/image/258106584/langan-thomas-page-11-us-southern-claims-commission-approved-claims-1871-1880.
7. Reginald M Coffey, *The American Dominicans: A History of Saint Joseph's Province* (Saint Martin de Porres Guild, 1970), 335.
8. *Tennessee Register*, April 24, 1959; see also Peter J. Meaney, OSB, "Valiant Chaplain of the Bloody Tenth," *Tennessee Historical Quarterly* 41, no. 1 (Spring 1982).

9. The Confederate Conscription Act of 1862 was the first military draft in American history and was signed into law by CSA president Jefferson Davis on April 16, 1862.

10. Wooten, *Johnsonville*, chapter 5.

11. Meaney, "Valiant Chaplain."

12. "Neither Blue nor Gray—Dominican Chaplains in the Civil War," Dominican Friars Province of St. Joseph, Nov. 4, 2012, https://opeast.org/2012/11/neither-blue-nor-gray-dominican-chaplains-in-the-civil-war.

13. Robert J. Miller, *Faith of the Fathers: The Comprehensive History of Catholic Chaplains in the Civil War* (Notre Dame Press, 2025).

14. Miller, *Faith of the Fathers.*

15. "Rev Fr Emmeran Bliemel (1831–1864)," Find a Grave, https://www.findagrave.com/memorial/8953/emmeran-bliemel.

16. Gretchen Keiser, "Priest Chaplain Who Died in Decisive Civil War Battle Remembered," *Georgia Bulletin*, September 5, 2014, https://georgiabulletin.org/news/2014/09/priest-chaplain-died-decisive-civil-war-battle-remembered/.

CHAPTER 8

1. Fr. George Flanigen's note about St. John the Evangelist, in the Flanigen Papers Archive at Aquinas College, and St. Mary of the Seven Sorrows 125th Anniversary booklet.

2. Cedar Knob would subsequently be known as Campbell's Hill after Judge G. W. Campbell and then, in 1843, Capitol Hill after the land was sold to the State of Tennessee for the location of the state capitol.

3. *Nashville Banner* and *Nashville Whig*, March 28, 1928.

4. O'Daniel, *The Father of the Church*, 210–300.

5. "1823 Nashville Toll Bridge Site - Trail of Tears National Historic Trail," Native History Association, https://nativehistoryassociation.org/tollbridge.php.

6. "Holy Rosary Cathedral Historical Marker," Historical Marker, February 7, 2023, https://www.hmdb.org/m.asp?m=36240.

7. Bishop Whelan's 1863 report to Diocese of Nashville, found in the Diocese of Nashville Archives.

8. George J. Flanigen, ed. *Catholicity in Tennessee: A Sketch of Catholic Activities in the State, 1541–1937* (Ambrose Printing Co., 1937), 47.

9. *Nashville Union and American*, Saturday, April 16, 1870.

10. Letter from E.F. Calahan to Fr. Larkin, 1909, Orengo files.

CHAPTER 9

1. *The Freeman's Journal*, March 25, 1865

2. John Morris, "Letter: to Rev. D. J. Kennedy, November 11, 1916," Orengo files.

3. John Morris. "Letter: to Victor F. O'Daniel, September 6, 1903," Orengo files.

4. John Morris, "1937 Homily at the Cathedral of the Incarnation in Nashville," Orengo files.

5. New York, US, Emigrant Saving Bank Records, 1850–1883, New York Public Library, via Ancestry.com.

6. "United States: Life Expectancy 1860 2020" | statista, https://www.statista.com/statistics/1040079/life-expectancy-united-states-all-time/.

7. Victor O'Daniel notes, Orengo files; "Smith Farmhouse Historical Marker," Historical Markers, https://www.hmdb.org/m.asp?m=151781.

8. "Immaculate Conception Catholic Church - Union City, Tennessee - About Us," Immaculate Conception Catholic Church, https://www.icuctn.org/about-us.

9. *Nashville Union and American*, April 13, 1867.

10. *Freeman's Journal*, February 6, 1869.

11. John Vidmar, "Mediterranean Missionaries and Their Contribution to the Early Province of St. Joseph, 1830–1870," *Inti: Revista de literatura hispánica*, no. 85/86 (2017): 22–31.

12. Vidmar, "Mediterranean Missionaries."

CHAPTER 10

1. McGraw et al., *Between the Rivers*, 37.

2. J. W. Wiley, *St. Mary's Church, Jackson, Tennessee: The Story of Catholicity in Jackson, Tennessee, from Earliest Times* (McCowat-Mercer Press,1951).

3. Wiley, *St. Mary's Church*.

4. Wiley, *St. Mary's Church*.

5. Sr. Mary Pius, "Letter to Fr. J. K. Larkin on May 24, 1909," Orengo files.

6. Flanigen, *Catholicity in Tennessee*, 133–34.

7. Saint Augustine stood until 1940, when it was sold and replaced with a new church name of Immaculate Conception.

8. Parish history records at St. Philip Catholic Church, Franklin, Tennessee.

9. *Nashville Union and American*, November 7, 1871.

10. McGraw et al., *Between the Rivers*, 48–49.

11. Luigi Orengo, "Letter: to Jennie Russell, February 9, 1888," Orengo files.

12. Orengo, "Letter: to Jennie Russell," Orengo files.

13. Orengo, "Letter to Jennie Russell," Orengo files.

14. Orengo, "Letter: to Johnnie Russell, April 16, 1885," Orengo files.

15. Orengo, "Letter: to Johnnie Russell, April 16, 1885," Orengo files.

16. "New York, Passenger Lists, 1820–1920," Entry for Louis Orengo, 1872, FamilySearch, https://www.familysearch.org/ark:/61903/1:1:QVR3-NHN9.

CHAPTER 11

1. Susan L. Gordon, "Epidemic Scourges in Tennessee," Tennessee State Library and Archives, https://sharetngov.tnsosfiles.com/tsla/exhibits/disasters/epidemics.htm.

2. "The Cholera in Tennessee," *New York Times*, July 11, 1873, https://timesmachine.nytimes.com/timesmachine/1873/07/11/113294665.html.

3. Father Lilly to Victor F. Daniel in "Saint Joseph's Province," Orengo files.

CHAPTER 12

1. *Maysville Bulletin*, April 12, 1877; *Maysville Republican*, April 14, 1877.

2. "HM King Umberto I of Italy." Henry Poole Savile Row, October 31, 2018. https://henrypoole.com/individual/king-umberto-i-of-italy/.

3. "Civic Hospitals of Sanremo," Sanremo Storia e Tradizioni, https://www.sanremostoria.it/en/the-town/urban-planning/palaces-and-building/215-civil-and-public-buildings/1036-civil-hospitals-of-sanremo.html.

4. The James Alphonsus McMaster Papers, University of Notre Dame, https://archives.nd.edu/cgi-bin/author.pl?c1883.xml+57.

5. *The Irish World and American Industrial Liberator* was a weekly newspaper published out of New York City.

6. A votive mass is mass said for a special intention that does not follow the Divine Office for that day.

EPILOGUE

1. Orengo, twenty-five years into his Tennessee missions as this point, appears to have misremembered his arrival year. He arrived in McEwen in 1849.

2. O'Daniel, *The Father of the Church*, 563.

BIBLIOGRAPHY

ARCHIVES CONSULTED

Archives at Curia Generalizia dei Domenicani at Santa Sabina, Aventino, Italy

Archives at Santa Maria Sopra Minerva in Rome, Italy

Aquinas College Library, Nashville, Tennessee — Flanigen Papers

Diocesan Archives, Archdiocese of Louisville, Louisville, Kentucky

Diocesan Archives, Diocese of Nashville, Nashville, Tennessee

James Alphonsus McMaster Papers, University of Notre Dame Archives, Notre Dame, Indiana

Madison County Public Records at the Madison County Archives, Jackson, Tennessee

Orengo Files, Dominican Province of St. Joseph, Washington, DC

Parish Archives at St. Mary of the Seven Sorrows, McEwen, Tennessee

Parish Archives at St. Patrick's Catholic Church, McEwen, Tennessee

Parish Archives at St. Peter's Catholic Church, Memphis, Tennessee

Tennessee State Library & Archives, Nashville, Tennessee

BIBLIOGRAPHY

Ahlstrom, Sydney E. *A Religious History of the American People*, vol. 1. Image Books, 1975.

Ash, Stephen A. *Middle Tennessee Transformed 1860–1870: War and Peace in the Upper South*. Louisiana State University Press, 1988.

Bradley, Kristen A. "A Tennessee Irish Picnic: Foodways and Complex Community Dynamics." PhD diss. University of Louisiana at Lafayette, 2014.

Campion, Msgr. Owen. "Andrew Johnson: Remembering a Champion of the Church." *Our Sunday Visitor*, January 17, 2020. https://www.oursundayvisitor.com/andrew-johnson-remembering-a-champion-of-the-church/.

Carey, Bill. "Ridesharing . . . 1800s Style." *The Tennessee Magazine*, November 1, 2022. https://www.tnmagazine.org/ridesharing-1800s-style/.

Caplinger, Christopher. "Yellow Fever Epidemics." *Tennessee Encyclopedia*, March 1, 2018. https://tennesseeencyclopedia.net/entries/yellow-fever-epidemics/.

Coffey, Reginald M. *The American Dominicans: A History of Saint Joseph's Province*. Saint Martin de Porres Guild, 1970.

Curran, Robert Emmett. *American Catholics and the Quest for Equality in the Civil War Era*. Louisiana State University Press, 2023.

Davenport, F. Garvin. *Cultural Life in Nashville on the Eve of the Civil War*. University of North Carolina Press, 1941.

Durkin, Mary Cabrini, and Mary Nona McGreal. *Always on Call: Samuel Mazzuchelli of the Order of Preachers, 1806–1864*. Éditions du Signe, 2000.

Elkins, Elizabeth. *We Should Soon Become Respectable: Nashville's Own Timothy Demonbreun*. Vanderbilt University Press, 2022.

Fieth, Kenneth. "Cumberland Compact." *Tennessee Encyclopedia*, March 1, 2018. http://tennesseeencyclopedia.net/entries/cumberland-compact/.

Flanigen, George J. *Catholicity in Tennessee: A Sketch of Catholic Activities in the State, 1541–1937*. Ambrose Printing Co., 1937.

Gibney, Laurence V., Jr. *The Church on Summit Hill: The Catholics of Knoxville and East Tennessee*. Immaculate Conception Church, 1986.

Gleason, Philip. "From an Indefinite Homogeneity: Catholic Colleges in Antebellum America." *The Catholic Historical Review* 94, no. 1 (January 1, 2008): 45–75.

Heller, Paul. "Montpelier's Secret Society: The Order of the Star-Spangled Banner." *Times Argus*, August 6, 2024. https://www.timesargus.com/news/local/montpelier-s-secret-society-the-order-of-the-star-spangled-banner/.

Higham, John. *Strangers in the Land: Patterns of American Nativism 1860–1925*. Atheneum, 1965.

Hood, Robin, Whit Styles, and Farrar Hood Cusamato. *Diocese of Nashville: A Family of Faith*. Grandin Hood Publishers, 2023.

Keane, James T. *Reading Culture Through Catholic Eyes: 50 Writers, Thinkers & Firebrands Who Challenge & Change Us*. Orbis Books, 2024.

Kuettner, Rev. Edward J. "Letter to Rev. John K. Larkin, July 7, 1909." Archives at St. Patrick's Church in McEwen.

Leith, Mary Joan. "The Crucifixion Conundrum and the Santa Sabina Doors." *Harvard Theological Review*, 2010.

Lehman, John. "Letter to Fr. George Flanigen, Feb. 10, 1967." The Flanigen Papers archive at Aquinas College Library.

Mazzuchelli, Samuel. *The Memoirs of Father Samuel Mazzuchelli*. Priory Press, 1967.

McGreal, Mary Nona. *The Order of Preachers in the United States: A Family History*, vol. 1. Editions du Signe, 2001.

McGraw, Joel William, Milton J. Guthrie, and Josephine King. *Between the Rivers: The Catholic Heritage of West Tennessee*. Catholic Diocese of Memphis; J.S. Sanders & Co., 1996.

Miller, Robert J. *Faith of the Fathers: The Comprehensive History of Catholic Chaplains in the Civil War*. University of Notre Dame Press, 2025.

O'Daniel, V. F. *The Father of the Church in Tennessee*. Dominicana, 1926.

O'Daniel, V. F. *The Dominican Province of Saint Joseph*. Holy Name Society, 1942.

O'Daniel, V. F. *The Right Rev. Edward Dominic Fenwick, OP.* Dominicana, 1920.

O'Daniel, V. F. *The First Two Dominican Priories in the United States*. Holy Name Society, 1947.

Pyburn, Eliza. "The Parish of McEwen, Tennessee." March 31–April 2, 1909. Archives at St. Patrick's Church in McEwen.

Starrs, Paul M. "The California Chronicle of Francis Sadoc Vilarrasa, OP, 1850–1874." *Catholic Historical Review*, 1952.

Stritch, Thomas. *The Catholic Church in Tennessee: The Sesquicentennial Story*. Catholic Center, 1987.

United States Work Projects Administration. *Slave Narratives: A Folk History of Slavery in the United States from Interviews with Former Slaves – Tennessee Narratives*. Project Gutenberg, 2006.

Vidmar, John. "Mediterranean Missionaries and Their Contribution to the Early Province of St. Joseph, 1830–1870." *Inti: Revista de literatura hispánica*, no. 85/86 (2017): 22–31. https://www.jstor.org/stable/45129655.

Wiley, J.W. *St. Mary's Church, Jackson, Tennessee*. McCowat-Mercer Press, 1951.

Wooten, Jerry T. *Johnsonville: Union Supply Operations on the Tennessee River and the Battle of Johnsonville, November 4–5, 1864*. Savas Beatie, 2021.

INDEX

Page numbers in *italic* refer to figures.